Dialectical Behaviour Therapy

An Essential Dbt Guide for Managing Intense Emotions

(A Guide to Overcoming Ptsd With Exercises for Skills and Tool Emotion Regulation)

Bryant Porter

Published By **Tyson Maxwell**

Bryant Porter

Dialectical Behaviour Therapy: An Essential Dbt Guide for Managing Intense Emotions (A Guide to Overcoming Ptsd With Exercises for Skills and Tool Emotion Regulation)

ISBN 978-1-998901-34-0

Legal & Disclaimer

The information contained in this ebook is not designed to replace or take the place of any form of medicine or professional medical advice. The information in this ebook has been provided for educational & entertainment purposes only.

The information contained in this book has been compiled from sources deemed reliable, and it is accurate to the best of the Author's knowledge; however, the Author cannot guarantee its accuracy and validity and cannot be held liable for any errors or omissions. Changes are periodically made to this book. You must consult your doctor or get professional medical advice before using any of the suggested remedies, techniques, or information in this book.

Table of contents

Chapter 1: Dialectical Conduct Therapy - What And Why? 1

Chapter 2: Building Willpower To Change 13

Chapter 3: Building Your Sense Of Mindfulness 23

Chapter 4: Building Your Distress Tolerance 47

Chapter 5: Building Your Emotional Regulation... 80

Chapter 6: Interpersonal Effectiveness .. 94

Chapter 7: Helping Somebody Else 103

Chapter 8: Dialectical Behavior Therapy For Teens 106

Chapter 9: Being Overweight Shouldn't Stop You From Being Happy With Your Body...................................... 163

Chapter 1: Dialectical Conduct Therapy - What And Why?

We'll begin this book out through asking a question that is important to the whole text: what is dialectical conduct remedy, and what blessings are there to the usage of it? We're moreover going to be taking a check a few special essential matters, which include what distinguishes dialectical behavior remedy from one-of-a-type well-known sorts of remedy which encompass cognitive conduct remedy.

Where does dialectical behavior remedy's information lie? The story starts offevolved offevolved in the Eighties with a disease called borderline person sickness.

Borderline persona disease is likewise known as emotionally risky character sickness, which tells you more or an entire lot less loads of what you need to recognize about the sickness. It can exceptional be described as an prolonged-habitual and deeply ingrained set of tendencies that revolve around a relevant feeling of vacancy and detachment, as well as a popular worry of being abandoned.

People who be afflicted by borderline character also commonly tend to have a completely unstable view of themselves and volatile emotions in wellknown. People who suffer from borderline personality sickness regularly may have a parallel trouble, which incorporates a history of substance abuse, despair, or eating problems like anorexia or bulimia. What's extra is that human beings who have borderline individual disorder are quite probably to die by way of suicide; in reality, one in ten human beings with borderline man or woman illness will die by using the use of their very very own hand.

The maximum difficult thing for treating human beings with borderline man or woman disorder became the reality that character issues have a tendency to be very hard to cope with with medicinal drug; their causes are not concrete and it's hard to pin them all the manner down to a novel motive that treatment can be made to cope with. It's more tough, too, at the same time as you hold in mind the fact that whilst distinct problems usually have easy effects on the thoughts, borderline person illness has no such clear impact at the brain that may be effortlessly mitigated by the usage of medication. While there may be evidence that it impacts a high-quality part of the mind, there's no diagnosed method to definitely affect the right purpose of borderline character illness in any effective way. Medication can fine absolutely be prescribed to soothe outer edge conditions however can't truely have an effect on the center state of affairs in any shape of significant manner.

What resulted changed into the number one shape of psychotherapy demonstrated to be usually powerful inside the treatment of borderline character sickness. However, it's additionally set up useful within the remedy of people with famous troubles like self-harming or suicidal thoughts.

This specific model of remedy works for those people in a way that most one-of-a-kind styles of treatment do no longer due to the fact it is based totally round getting the patients to increase their potential to alter every their feelings and their mind via assessing what honestly reasons them to experience the way they do, and what it's miles that they'll do so as to use it on themselves.

It does such through a set of diverse requirements supposed to isolate, examine, and overlook approximately about horrible thoughts without a doubt. To gain this, dialectical conduct remedy is classified into 4 extremely good modules which are finished in a cyclical way. These are as follows.

The first is mindfulness. Mindfulness is probably the maximum important building block of dialectical behavior remedy, and it's miles the element which precludes the whole lot else. Building mindfulness is really crucial. We'll be talking about mindfulness very in-depth in its respective financial ruin.

The 2d is distress tolerance. Distress tolerance refers in large part to one's capability to deal with things that distress them. This runs in opposition to the contemporary-day style in intellectual health remedies to try to change traumatic situations. For humans with irrational or self-poor notion patterns, the attempt to alternate those distressing conditions can be one of the topics which catalyze and get worse any individual's poor behaviors.

The 0.33 is emotional law. Emotional regulation offers with the capability for a person as a manner to apprehend and manage their emotions reactively, in addition to to deal with topics with a more diploma of detachment and objectivity. There are many particular strategies worried inside the building of emotional regulation skills.

The last is interpersonal effectiveness. Interpersonal effectiveness has to do with the capability of an man or woman to efficiently speak and address one of a kind humans. While people who be troubled by borderline person illness and related problems commonly are able to describe how a scenario want to be handled, they will be commonly not able to accomplish that while they're in the purpose pressure's seat, so to speak. They will clam up or motel to knee-jerk reactions in dealing with wonderful humans.

It is thru the biking of these 4 thoughts that one may additionally additionally accumulate the whole blessings of dialectical conduct treatment.

The middle of dialectical conduct treatment is primarily based at some point of the interplay among the therapist and the affected character. The therapist is supposed to be enormously supportive of the affected person, being reachable outside of remedy intervals if crucial as a way to offer consistent emotional help for the affected character. The affected individual is likewise intended to view the therapist as a friend in location of foe. In order to make this occur, the rationale of the therapist is to simply accept the affected individual's feelings on the equal time as additionally telling them that some of the matters they do are terrible and giving them steering as to how they may cope with matters in a better way.

The save you purpose of the classes is for the affected character to acquire what they could outline as a "existence sincerely simply really worth dwelling" through each the changing of contemporary behaviors and the development of latest behaviors.

So, with all of that during mind, one has to invite: with the focal point of dialectical behavior treatment being so closely geared towards the reputation quo of a courting between someone and a therapist, is it a practical approach to try to do it in your very very personal?

The easy solution is that positive, it's sensible. However, it is going to take a whole lot of paintings on your prevent. By the cease, although, you ought that allows you to use dialectical conduct remedy on the way to higher control your relationships, problems, and enormous malaise.

The reason of this ebook is to offer you the essential shape so that you're capable of do dialectical behavior remedy to your private; however, there may be a chapter reserved for assisting any character else the use of the method's in this ebook, such that you may act as their "therapist" as it had been. Be conscious that in case you're going to do such a element, you want to be mentally organized for irrespective of the patient also can throw at you. You ought to really be accepting of them, or they may no longer sense as though they have got a friend in the way. The worst case is that you genuinely eliminate their development. This is the ultimate problem that you need to do!

The Outline for Dialectical Behavior Therapy

So now it's come time; you understand what dialectical behavior treatment is and also you've determined that it's the first-rate direction of movement for you. What can you start doing that permits you to get the most out of this machine? What steps can you take in order to start integrating dialectical behavior treatment into your every day life?

The first issue you want to apprehend is that dialectical conduct remedy doesn't try to push everything on you proper away. Rather, the approach is primarily based spherical durations wherein a sure one of the four methodologies within the lower back of dialectical conduct treatment are practiced.

It is, in overall, a six-month application. This software can also additionally additionally then be repeated over a long time body until the affected person feels cushty using and maintaining the abilities that they've advanced.

One also can separate this system into three outstanding -month blocks. All of those blocks start out with a two-week emphasis on mindfulness and mindfulness constructing techniques. The competencies advanced in the direction of the opportunity periods ought to be maintained but need to not be without a doubt the popularity. There is a six week reputation length after every -week mindfulness consultation so you can consciousness on one of the three other aspects of dialectical behavior remedy depending upon the current block of this gadget.

The first block is based totally throughout the emotional regulation capabilities and could cope with building the capabilities which the affected person maximum needs that permits you to correctly adjust their feelings.

The 2d block is based totally across the understanding of putting up with distress and will deal with retaining and growing the affected man or woman's capability to tolerate distress. This block is rather essential to the development of the affected individual and is a top a part of the whole tool.

The 0.33 block is based spherical constructing the patient's capability to effectively communicate themselves to unique humans and maintain their interpersonal relationships. This block is meant to build stability within the affected person's surroundings and is also important.

As the affected character, you need to region emphasis on being able to correctly navigate all of those abilities. If you're running with a person else, you need to be checking in and making sure that you are blockading out and maintaining interest on each of those competencies in my opinion. Managing the development via every of those abilties through the improvement of an effective timetable is distinctly critical to the overall progress of whoever is attempting to benefit from the remedy method; all the elements are of exceptional importance and priority need to be located on acting out all of them.

In every of the following chapters, we're going to be discussing the movements that you can take so that it will workout all of those at the same time as the time comes and construct your skills in popular. Much of that is most with out problems accomplished with both a knowledgeable therapist or any individual who's willing to paste with the resource of your side as you try to do the whole lot interior this guide. However, it's far very sensible which you are able to deliver it out on your personal so long as you assemble the willpower important to reap this.

Chapter 2: Building Willpower To Change

One component that may be instead difficult even as searching for to make a top notch change for your self is clearly taking the first step ahead. Once you do take step one and begin to set up some shape of routine for yourself, you agree into it mentally and it turns into plenty less difficult. It moreover has a bent to grow to be even a whole lot much less complex as you press in advance with it. However, even as you're honestly starting out, it can be tough to absolutely cement so that you can inside your self.

Understand that the conduit to real and actionable trade springs forth from indoors your self. In reality, while working with humans through the dialectical conduct technique, therapists recognize that the first step is to make certain that the affected person is best and wants to get higher.

13

Do understand that this ebook has a financial disaster dedicated to the concept of running with any person else through dialectical conduct remedy, so if you're seeking to artwork with any man or woman that you realise and care about, this ebook does offer for you. However, the primary numerous chapters are extra based totally around the idea of running with yourself.

So, with all of that during mind, how can you are taking the number one steps toward recognizing that some thing wishes to alternate? The first is thru an honest evaluation of your moves and your behaviors.

The first element you need to recognize is that if there's regular tension on your life, there's a risk that you are a common denominator. There isn't anything incorrect with expertise this, despite the fact that. We all convey a big amount of luggage sooner or later of our lives and statistics how that luggage maintains to have an effect on you is a as an opportunity massive part of the restoration way.

Recognize that there can be now not something wrong with looking for to trade for the better. Healthiness is a first-rate element. You should be actively seeking out this commonplace wellness and fitness. Although it cannot appear like it proper now, the form of happiness that you're trying is every actual and achievable for clearly everyone, even yourself.

The first step to getting there, even though, is to admit to yourself which you need to change. If you apprehend that topics are going poorly, you need to analyze the matters which is probably taking place to you and in reality attempt to see what thing you're playing in them.

Many people revel in just like the 2d that they admit to themselves that they will make a exchange, their complete lifestyles is probably thrown out of whack. Sometimes they feel like their current-day lifestyles is simply too cemented to sincerely make an powerful trade possible. Both of those viewpoints are explicitly wrong, despite the fact that.

The reality is that while some important shifts is probably critical to your existence so as so you can end up a happier and additional wholesome human, the good sized majority of those are going to be coming from interior your self - they may be now not, necessarily, subjects which arise round you.

I assume that the notable element approximately all of it's miles that maximum of the exchange comes from a shift to your extremely-contemporary angle. The weight this is lifted while you start to drift a long way from those subjects which fog your modern notion, on this shape of manner that you could begin to expect and act rationally, is a completely lovely element; you'll feel like a modern-day person.

The biggest part of all of this comes with in reality trying to make a trade. Understand that having that actual preference for alternate method constantly which you are able to get keep of subjects approximately yourself, even the hard things, which might be generally difficult a good way to get hold of.

These subjects may be accurate or terrible, too; as an example, if you be concerned with the useful resource of despair, it can be which you want to truely receive that some of the irrational mind and conceptions aren't always right. On the opportunity hand, if you be stricken by a chunk of situational narcissism and will be inclined to displace blame as a protection mechanism, you can discover that you need to simply accept that you may, in fact, do incorrect - even if your narcissism is a safety mechanism inner itself.

The toughest a part of all of that is the truth that intellectual contamination simply, in the end, isn't always lessen and dry. Working with highbrow contamination can display very difficult in fact, due to the truth in truth everyone's intellectual contamination will arise in a way which is essentially one-of-a-kind, despite the fact that the illnesses study comparable paths and percentage positive attributes. Therefore, it may be pretty hard to honestly get out of these rhythms and determine out what's proper and isn't, further to what will be simply proper for you and what gained't.

Be aware, despite the fact that, that all of the alternate you need will in the long run be summoned from interior yourself. You ought to summon the choice to make a actual and actual effort to trade.

You can and most possibly will enjoy fulfillment the usage of this method, however you need to be open to trade. The massive kicker is power of thoughts. It's going to take pretty some energy of will a first rate manner to navigate this form of remedy including you're going to want to.

When you be bothered by means of the issues that dialectical behavior remedy is meant to restoration, schooling this quantity of strength of will may be as a substitute hard in and of itself. It isn't, however, now not possible. Your thoughts is continuously frayed or jumping anywhere within the area, or on occasion you've got were given rapid and insufferable temper swings. Even if not the ones, it's viable that you react to conditions in self-destructive ways that you don't pretty apprehend. Perhaps you don't even understand what you do or why, however you recognise that it's having a horrible effect for your relationships.

The factor of dialectical behavior treatment is ultimately that will help you pinpoint, understand, after which impact exchange in regard to these troubles. In order to achieve this, you furthermore mght need to be inclined to admit to your self that the ones problems exist within the first region. This is the vital first step to improvement. Understand this in advance than you are taking any similarly movement; achieving the give up of the street to achievement calls for that you strain it nicely. Driving it properly right right here manner which you want to be prepared to really be given which you are not perfect; you may make mistakes, you can have beside the thing or hurtful idea styles, you may do subjects that you ought not do. Accepting that you'll obtain this is in reality pivotal within the grand scheme of finding out your highbrow troubles.

Another essential trouble is fending off getting discouraged. Remember that this software particularly lasts for 6 months and is meant to be cyclical such that it could be repeated as vital. Your outcomes are not going to be right now, and chances are that you're going to regress now and again too. Your technique for dealing with this wants to revolve round accepting the reality that no longer the whole thing is going to transport in a linear style.

Realize which you're going to reduce to rubble once in a while, and additionally that you're in the long run not going to make a heap of development unexpectedly. Consider it like losing weight. When you lose quite a few weight, it may be difficult to in fact verify how an entire lot weight you've out of place, due to the truth you spot your self every day. The fine time that this sort of component surely will become apparent is if you have a look at your self to an vintage image or if a person brings up the truth that you've lost weight.

It's an awful lot the identical proper right here. While a whole lot of the intellectual changes received't be without delay maximum critical, the changes you're making to your mind-set as an entire will result in the improvement of a miles greater healthful fashionable idea technique over the longer term.

Chapter 3: Building Your Sense Of Mindfulness

The first a part of strolling with dialectical behavior treatment lies in education a sure center set of skills. These abilties are going to be critical to your improvement within the technique as an entire. Working with dialectical conduct treatment in your very own may be hard, however with attempt you can make maximum of the thoughts arise for your self.

The first idea you need to artwork on building is mindfulness. Mindfulness is a vital part of dialectical behavior remedy further to constructing your capability to address harmful mind in famous. So, what exactly is mindfulness?

In the development of dialectical behavior remedy, concepts were synthesized into one cohesive unit from across the entire global. Some of those necessities came from the East. One such idea is that of mindfulness. Mindfulness is a difficult idea to offer an reason behind inside the beginning. It basically revolves for the duration of the idea of being present inside the given 2d.

In order to unique mindfulness, it's probably less difficult to don't forget the manner that your thoughts works at any given second. Much of the time, you're no longer actively thinking about what is going on inside the advise time; often, you'll input right right right into a shape of autopilot mode. Upon entering this autopilot mode, you usually generally generally tend to first off lose music of the mind which you want to be having. However, unique mind will be inclined to come to the forefront as nicely - you may start considering the past or worrying about the destiny.

This is a wonderfully ordinary response, don't worry; in reality all people passes their time thinking about a few component aside from the present except they specially train themselves not to. However, the Eastern religions had been proper in their assessment of this workout: it to begin with is illogical, given that the simplest thing which might also moreover occur is the triumphing, and it secondly is a conduit to vain struggling.

Breaking this dependancy is essential, despite the fact that. People never in reality don't forget how silly it's miles to be thinking about some detail aside from the existing.

More than that, despite the fact that, mindfulness is crucial in education yourself to allow thoughts come and bypass. The potential of spotting a belief after which liberating that concept is pretty crucial to every person trying to take manipulate in their mind. Much of the time, you'll count on a few element irrational and then start to latch onto that concept. Going in the direction of this grain and letting the concept be let loose is critical to the whole lot of dialectical behavior remedy similarly to creating ahead development as a person in significant.

Mindfulness is the smooth concept of being privy to your thoughts. There are a few various things that you may do so that you can educate it. We're going initially looking on the idea a piece bit greater closely earlier than we get into the training of mindfulness reflexes, although.

Why would possibly likely mindfulness be vital, and the way could probably you benefit from it?

Mindfulness is essential in constructing the ability to allow your self to simultaneously get hold of the feelings that you feel each time you try to disrupt a few aspect unfavorable behavior you could have developed, in addition to supplying you with the talent set vital to transport earlier and allow the mind not to problem you as masses as they usually may.

A big part of borderline man or woman disease, similarly to suicidal ideation, substance abuse, and numerous considered one of a kind problems, lies inside the fashion of irrational response. This fashion exists as a characteristic of recognizing some type of problem - whether or not or now not actual or imaginary - then responding in an irrational manner to that problem. Mindfulness is part of permitting yourself to apprehend what's and isn't rational, then deal with it in a responsible manner.

If, as an example, you find out it specially tough to really be given that anyone isn't going to barren area you, then you may discover the capacity to interest on what you're doing at that given second and famend what you're feeling in a passive way without reacting to it specially useful.

Mindfulness in psychology is normally taken into consideration as a thoroughfare as a way to begin to apprehend yourself and your reactions, similarly to a way of concurrently heading off unique trains of emotional reaction: each the avoidance of vital emotion, or the over assessment of and overreaction to emotion. In either case, mindfulness allows you to be actively engaged in conjunction with your feelings in an entire manner similarly to to be actively disengaged out of your feelings thru putting your self extra inside the sphere of the real worldwide in desire to setting apart your self in a sphere of horrific emotion.

Indeed, a as an alternative massive part of dialectical behavior treatment lies inside the strive of the affected person to rid themselves of emotional struggling to the excellent quantity which they likely can.

So, shifting similarly, we're going to begin talking approximately the development of mindfulness within the context of dialectical behavior treatment. Mindfulness is split into amazing education: what abilities and the manner abilities. Both of these are imagined to help the surrender customer with information and carrying out mindfulness because it were.

What

The whats are focused spherical solution the query of what we're seeking to do even as appealing ourselves in mindfulness exercise. What are the forestall desires? What are we in truth looking to perform?

The first detail that we're trying to perform is the capability to take a look at our emotions in addition to the matters round us. In this potential, mindfulness is supposed to permit us to accomplish that during a nonjudgmental and pretty aim manner. That is to say that declaration within the context of mindfulness ought to preferably be instead indifferent. If you experience especially close to your situation, then you surely definately're feeling a way that is usually counter to what need to be your "intention" in mindfulness education and exploration.

This isn't to say that you want to actively track out, but that you have to exercise the art work of seeing yourself in a greater indifferent manner. For instance, in a scenario wherein you'll likely in any other case deflect blame onto someone else as a knee-jerk response, try and take a step lower back and check the scenario objectively. What befell?

Mindfulness is useful in permitting you to each have a have a look at the state of affairs in an active and indifferent manner in addition to providing you with the readability of mind which you want with a purpose to both cope with or gather the situation in a vast manner.

One core recognition of dialectical behavior remedy lies within the idea of accepting difficult conditions. Realize that in those forms of conditions, whilst you may have a minimal impact, there are numerous greater elements than just you on the coronary coronary heart of them. What this in the end manner is that no matter some detail you'll be looking for to do or a few thing you may think, there's simplest quite a few a hand you can have in any precise element. Moreover, resistance for your fears and your knee jerk reactions inside the ones kinds of conditions regularly best exacerbates the problem. Dialectical behavior remedy is based totally totally round willing yourself to in reality accept situations in choice to seeking to change them.

Mindfulness is a key part of recognition, due to the truth if you are being actively aware, you're figuring out which you are best able to trade that that you are able to exchange. You are conscious of your hand in the situation similarly to - extra importantly - your response to the state of affairs. While stylish passivity isn't practical and also will be unstable, you want to apprehend that general reaction may be surely as dangerous if not even greater, specially whilst you already will be inclined to overreact and be risky inside the first area.

The author of dialectical conduct therapy recommends that one develops what she called a Teflon mind, which is largely the capacity to allow matters and emotions get up with out them sticking round for your thoughts. In this philosophy lies the crux of mindfulness: active participation within the 2nd in location of letting yourself get slowed down with unnecessary matters.

Mindfulness should have many components, but from second to second, you want to come to be as aware as feasible of these things which you understand through your senses, together with your senses being usually described as imaginative and prescient, feeling, being attentive to, tasting, and smelling. Your cause is to take in as an entire lot as you possibly can from those property and be without a doubt privy to what is occurring in the gift second.

The subsequent vital what of mindfulness is the capability to provide an reason for. Description is an surely vital capability. You need to advantage the potential to mention the topics that you are looking. It's right right right here that description profits the maximum critical a part of its utility.

Description isn't clean to begin with, especially because you're seeking to describe topics without passing judgment on them. Indeed, gaining the capability to give an explanation for subjects with out explicitly passing judgment on them is of paramount significance inside the pursuit of in the end being able to be completely attuned in your surroundings and going for walks inner it. More than that, it's of big importance to the cease motive of being capable of method your very own feelings in a nonjudgmental way.

Behaving nonjudgmentally is a capacity all in itself, and it's some issue you're looking to without a doubt ingrain with the description potential. You may not be honestly clean on simply what description technique on this context; without a doubt it honestly refers to your capability to select out the developments about the matters which you take a look at spherical you or inner you and then speakme them efficaciously in a nonjudgmental manner.

The powerful utilization of this capacity can result in a big quantity of progress being made in the different sides as properly.

The final what of mindfulness rests in participation. Participation is ready being actually lively inside the second. If you're performing some aspect, participation asks which you be actually targeted and concerned with that hobby. This harkens returned to the concept of mindfulness to start with being a tool of Eastern philosophy to benefit whole and absolute recognition of any given second.

Note that mindfulness is not clean, and neither is the capability of participation and being conscious. These are, in truth, topics that you're going to have to train through the years. Don't be indignant if you discover it tough at the start to live clearly and completely centered at the responsibilities accessible. Just exercise bringing your self once more to them in a conscious way.

What matters are you capable of do in an effort to bring your self once more to the hobby reachable? Good question! The awesome techniques for restoring your conscious characteristic are those in which you reputation on the world round you. If you find out your self dropping cognizance, carry your self to hobby and recall the matters which correspond in your five senses. Describe them internally. Once you've achieved so, you'll locate that your element of consciousness is regularly restored and also you'll maximum likely be able to pass again for your middle attention in your pastime at any given 2nd.

Remember to use the moment as your tool. This is one of the most vital elements about participation and mindfulness in trendy. There will in no way be however that this is, irrespective of the fact that that it virtually is will always impacted via manner of the beyond and the future. Because of that, you could typically use what's in an effort to supply your self once more to specializing in what is.

If you discover your thoughts floating off at the same time as you're doing some thing, use your senses or unique mindfulness strategies you observe about or growth on the way to carry your self again to in which you need to be.

Mindfulness is a subject, like anything else. It's going to be tough for you to accumulate the functionality to continuously rein in your attention and deal with one specific detail. However, similar to each other challenge, the extra you exercising at it, the higher you'll turn out to be at it.

How

Now that we've referred to the whats of mindfulness, it's time that we start to talk about the hows of mindfulness. These are the essential techniques in which you want to continually method mindfulness such that you can start to actively revise a number of the toxic styles you've advanced up to now on your lifestyles. Recognizing those critical hows is probably important for you moving ahead as properly.

These hows answer the question of the way you're supposed to be drawing close your mindfulness wearing activities. In that, at the same time as you're searching out to exquisite your mindfulness technique, those will display particularly fruitful on your challenge.

The first how is nonjudgmentally, as in I want to method mindfulness nonjudgmentally. As we referred to in advance on this financial catastrophe, the nonjudgmental method to mindfulness is vital. This is because it permits you to shed any conduct of judgment that you already have.

Moreover, at the same time as you do need to talk your mind, with the useful resource of putting them via a nonjudgmental clean out, you permit your self to evaluate topics in a totally purpose manner, or at least goal internal a tremendous positive.

Additionally, even as you act nonjudgmentally, it makes you as a person an extended way greater agreeable. One of your issues may be to every inform yourself or any character else some thing in this kind of way that it makes it come off in a awful manner and getting to know to govern that is sincerely crucial to persevering with to your mindfulness adventure.

More than that, even as you parent with mindfulness and also you act nonjudgmentally, you lessen your hazard of ruining your awareness through getting caught up on your prejudgments or judgments of a few issue. This method which you're much more likely to stay targeted and on mission than you may be otherwise. This could make a quite large difference on your capability to in reality perform your mindfulness exercise.

The 2d how is that you want to workout mindfulness one-mindfully. What this means is that you want to hone your capability to stay focused in on one factor in preference to letting your awareness slide from assignment depend to venture rely aimlessly.

The principle purpose of this how is that while you are as focused as you need to be, you may ideally hold yourself from slipping into your feelings and could therefore have a much easier time regulating your emotions and staying genuinely rational in place of potentially performing irrational.

Keeping your self of 1 mind and on one undertaking approach that you are capable of higher capable of permit yourself to run with out the undertaking of your emotional mind. Indeed, having the potential to break out the hindering presence of the emotional mind is considered to be a essential part of dialectical behavior treatment.

Maintaining your state of one-mind turns into a long way much less complicated as time is going on and you determine with the requirements increasingly. Just bear in mind which you need to maintain doing what you can so that you can maintain it. It will broaden over the years, like a muscle. This furthermore approach that early on it's going to tire you out to preserve your attention for as extended as you're seeking to. Don't fear, no matter the fact that, that may be a normal reaction to the heightened quantity of consciousness.

The objective of all of that is to beautify your attention, don't neglect about. Concentration is a very essential part of mindfulness and the functionality to pay attention and manipulate your mind is a likewise essential aspect.

The very last how is efficiently, as in You want to workout mindfulness effectively. In that, there is a lot of meaning carried. Essentially, the point is that there may be no right manner or wrong manner to exercise mindfulness for the ones purposes necessarily; there's no need to get stuck up in some shape of pseudo-non secular dogma about the right or wrong way to remember - there are real religions for that.

Instead, this how is about recognizing that mindfulness manner hundreds of factors to a variety of human beings; it has both a historical religious because of this, a intellectual because of this, and a couple different meanings that it's taken over time. In the prevent, maximum of the meanings meet on the general definition of mindfulness even though the precise goals of that form of mindfulness range.

In that, there isn't always a incorrect way to build up mindfulness. Rather, your cognizance should be on genuinely undertaking it. Therefore, don't worry about doing the right or incorrect element. Just do what works and is powerful; in essence, do what you want to an outstanding manner to grow to be conscious. This is the path ahead for proper mindfulness.

The goal of mindfulness training is to certainly come up with the potential to recollect in a holistic manner, such that you may preserve in thoughts in as proper of a way viable. This will help you benefit control of your thoughts and your reactions, similarly to your chosen mood and stability.

Remember that you are actively fighting in competition to the modern-day, too. This element will in no way be always smooth as it's a hint bit ingrained into you to be emotionally unstable or otherwise have some form of hassle that you need to deal with; understand this and recognize that those problems very well can also obtain proper all of the way right down to even the quantity of your genetics.

However, on the same time because it obtained't ever be easy or a hundred% effective, it will purpose you success in the long run as you advantage greater strength over your feelings and your reactions. For this motive, you want to recollect that even if you don't see fulfillment one hundred%, you still are seeking out success, and also you're looking for it in plenty smaller quantities than a hundred%. Seek out your ability specially to live conscious even as matters get tough, in addition on your capability to regain your consciousness at the same time as you lose it.

In different terms, mindfulness is a marathon, now not a dash. You don't want to anticipate maximum vital development. You really need to assume that you can make small strides, although ordinary, and that the ones strides will assist you to higher address, examine, and address the problems that you're seeking to address within the first location.

With all of that out of the manner, it's time that we start talking approximately the way you certainly construct mindfulness. After all, we've spent a long time talking about the manner you need to workout mindfulness and what you need to do, however we haven't quite said how you can really assemble the talent of mindfulness.

The method that I'm going to suggest particularly is meditation. Meditation has been used for millennia to collect mindfulness abilities. While it may seem a bit hokey before everything, meditation has been tested in highbrow contexts to have a net first-class highbrow effect on people who do it frequently.

There is a manner to meditation, even though. Actually, there are various. The remarkable advice that I can come up with is to move on YouTube and are looking for out guided mindfulness meditation movies. These will stroll you through the technique of developing your mindfulness and present day revel in of popularity.

Meditation can be hard at the begin and may seem boring, but through the years you'll advantage a more and extra appreciation for the exercise itself similarly to a greater capability to genuinely perform meditation inside the capacity that you need to for the quantity of time which you want to. Stick with it, due to the fact this is the way you assemble mindfulness.

Stay present, live alert, and live inside the second. This is the aspect of the mindfulness training.

Chapter 4: Building Your Distress Tolerance

Distress tolerance is a without a doubt important talent and, sadly, it's one that many humans with borderline personality sickness and related temper/emotional issues appear to lack. This doesn't suggest that every one is out of place, but. Much of your reactions to things comes from a combination of observed behaviors and the environment spherical you. By relearning your methodology for processing and managing feelings, you may truely begin to rebuild your potential to tolerate distress.

Dialectical behavior remedy differs in large component from unique mainstream treatment techniques in that it locations a instead large emphasis at the functionality of the man or woman to deal with distress, which incorporates trauma, situation, and typically stressful occasions. In some times, they will absolutely lack the capacity to rationalize in a wholesome manner why excellent topics are going on to them, in addition to why they will be the manner that they'll be. Other remedy strategies will be inclined to vicinity an emphasis on subjects along with preserving the problems or how one might also additionally have a proactive effect on them.

The reason that dialectical behavior remedy places an emphasis on accepting matters in place of creating a proactive alternate is because of the truth people who might be helped with the aid of dialectical behavior remedy are often the kind to overcompensate while they may be seeking to assert issues in their lifestyles. They may additionally have an emotional overreaction or any wide type of one-of-a-kind problems in response to a given stimulus. This is in evaluation to the normal reaction to overwhelming stimuli, which is to be burdened and probably stay stagnant till a clear route is given for them.

Because of this, masses of attention is located in dialectical behavior treatment on no longer allowing demanding stimuli to area an emotional burden on you. In precise terms, permitting it to not unsettle your waters too much.

The capability to cope with disturbing situations is really paramount in the improvement of a glad and healthful way of existence. You can't expect to be satisfied in case you don't have a ordinary, efficient, and healthy way of managing emotional trauma and great misery. There's a noticeably amazing threat that the purpose you're pursuing this route in the first location is because of the fact you've got a tough time managing your emotions as they come.

We'll talk more about managing emotions in an express way within the following financial catastrophe, despite the fact that. This financial ruin is more approximately handling the situations which create the feelings. Therefore, the center of this economic damage goes to be growing talents which can be essential for the emotional improvement of you as a person. If you follow the general recommendations referred to in this bankruptcy, you're going to locate yourself capable of thousands more often deal with situations which assignment you emotionally in a accountable manner.

The first part of this bankruptcy is available in sincerely accepting what goes on round you. We mentioned this inside the first economic damage, but it will become seriously essential proper right here. Many people have the crucial initial response to try to block out, alternate, or definitely reject the element this is taking area to or spherical them. This is innately an risky reaction mechanism, and also you want to try to avoid it as a wonderful deal as possible.

The aspect you want to apprehend is that no matter how an awful lot you need it to, blocking off out or seeking to exchange a scenario that is from your fingers often obtained't do something to honestly exchange it. Sometimes, things seem. Accepting this isn't a quitter mentality; searching for to reject it is a quitter mentality, because it approach which you aren't as plenty due to the fact the mission that's within the the front of you.

Often, humans increase this mentality of self-rejection as a reaction to important stimuli. To have that response of in search of to change or reject a state of affairs manner that you don't suppose which you are reduce out to upward push up to the scenario. Part of dialectical conduct remedy consists of considering what motives you to revel in this way and the manner you could avoid those triggers.

The author of dialectical behavior remedy has defined a number of techniques through which you may start to workout one-of-a-kind tracts which can be beneficial in the development of talents for misery tolerance. You need to practice the ones as an lousy lot as you can on your day after day lifestyles such that you can begin to intuitively use them even as the want arises.

Review those every day even as you're within the distress tolerance block so that you can firmly cement them into your mind. Also try to supply them with you in a single way or every one of a kind so that you can bear in mind what steps to take at the same time as you need any of the given gadgets of movements.

The first set of movements that have been superior are strategies of distraction. These are used so that after a distasteful emotion or situation comes up, you can begin to distract yourself and divert your interest faraway from it in a efficient way. This will beneficial useful resource you in assisting you to address emotional reaction. This furthermore goes hand in hand together with your mindfulness workout due to the reality the focusing capability which you boom while operating with mindfulness will will will permit you to fast* draw your hobby a few different place and deal with the topics which may be taking location internal your head.

You can keep in mind the ones movements through the acronym ACCEPTS. The letters inside the acronym spell out some top notch key mind.

The first key idea is sports activities. When you want to distract your self from a few aspect it is happening, try and divert your hobby within the direction of some thing else which you surely enjoy. This will absorb your power for a efficient and fantastic emotional revel in in place of one in order to purpose you to sense negatively and probably even helpless.

The subsequent key idea is contribution. Instead of focusing on yourself and the subjects happening to you on your immediate location, cognizance as an opportunity on how you may help out others or the human beings round you. Use it slow and resources and competencies with a purpose to make human beings round you feel better. This additionally has the more advantage that it will make you enjoy together with you're a better and additional green person than you probably did in advance than, so that you can decorate your degree of productiveness and your giant feeling of self-worth. This has a reflexive gain in that it starts to make you cost your self and experience slightly higher.

The next key idea which you need to cognizance on constructing within the ACCEPTS distraction technique is comparisons. Really, this idea is all about your thoughts-set. Compare yourself every to how others are feeling similarly to the progress that you've made up to now. While you aren't in a excellent characteristic at that 2d, consider that some people available are starving or homeless or worse. This isn't alleged to condescend; it's supposed to make you understand that as bad as subjects are, you aren't at rock bottom. More crucial than that, even though, is the potential to take inventory of your intellectual state and feature a take a look at in that you're to in that you've were given been. Since dialectical behavior therapy is prepared slow improvement as a person, your entire purpose is to collect upon yourself over time. Recognizing that you've made improvement can be a high-quality manner to make yourself revel in which includes you're at the right tune.

The following idea is emotions. This idea is set making yourself enjoy precise emotions than what you're currently feeling. Watch or do a little factor that makes you chortle or enjoy glad; participate in a hobby that makes you sense which include you're in a distinct headspace than you normally do; do something you may on the way to make yourself experience in a specific manner in preferred. This will offer you with the intellectual place that you want an excellent manner to positioned your self in a higher headspace.

After that, you want to exercise push away. This idea is about being able to positioned your state of affairs out of your thoughts for a while. This additionally goes hand in hand together at the side of your mindfulness exercise. Being capable of push matters far from you in phrases of your attitude is of paramount significance in being capable of live conscious and on pinnacle of things of your emotional reaction to superb situations. While a state of affairs may be far from apt or most incredible, your capacity to take that state of affairs and push it from your line of sight is going to be highly beneficial to you as you bypass in advance.

The capability after that is mind. In essence, use the exercise that you've evolved as a way to strain yourself to think about some thing else. Clear your mental dual carriageway of visitors so you can break out the jam, then cruise proper on via in a few thing that you feel snug and glad considering, or some component that truly takes a whole lot of mind electricity and consciousness for you.

The expertise following this, and the final idea that you want to exercise, is sensation. Sensations is ready locating subjects that could make you feel superb to the way you do right now. These are matters which have particularly sturdy and visceral emotional reactions that you may't virtually withstand. Try, for instance, specifically surprisingly spiced snacks or very frigid showers. Both of these will permit your frame to have a pressure reaction to a few component else and will occupy your mind for a bit. The genuine judgment is essentially the same as pinching your self while you stub your toe or hit your head so that you can divert your ache to some thing less painful. It's a actual know-how, and it's something which you want to increase. Plan for the usage of this skills, due to the truth it can be mainly beneficial to you.

Those thoughts define the primary basis of the accepts distraction approach. A colorful concept might be to region they all on be conscious playing playing cards and summarize them, then refresh your self every morning while you awaken and each night time time earlier than you go to mattress while you're doing all your distress tolerance block. These will help you in developing tolerance abilities for distasteful or worrying situations.

Another element that you need to focus on is locating a way to soothe your self. This is a concept called self-soothing, and it's specifically essential in dialectical behavior therapy. Essentially, this is all about locating processes that you could be type and comforting to your self.

We aren't imagined to run all of the time and in no manner have an opportunity to destress. You are imagined to have intervals of enjoyment time and simplicity. These are intended to help you with decompressing and unloading. Allowing yourself time to do that is vital because it we can also want in your thoughts reset to a piece of a clean kingdom.

Many people who have extant emotional troubles regularly experience that they're exacerbated by means of way of being in excessive strain environments and not allowing themselves the possibility to certainly decompress and lighten up. While this received't clear up all your emotional issues immediately, it could truely help you in processing them at the same time as you're out and about. Remembering that you have the possibility to destress at a later detail inside the day also can make it much less complex to take at the severa stresses of any given day, too. Don't be afraid to set time apart for yourself.

What precisely want to you be doing in this time? This is this sort of matters in which the selection in reality is yours. There is not any proper or incorrect trouble to be doing. Much just like the final rule of rneditation, the real aim right here is sincerely to be powerful: do what works for you!

There are many diverse things that you could discover soothes you. For instance, deliver your self time to take a bath at night time time, to take a look at literature of your favorite fashion, or to paintings on some form of hobby or mission. In effect, just be type to yourself. Allow your self the possibility to loosen up. Know that there's no longer a few component wrong with taking time to yourself. This is an essential a part of the distress tolerance block, so make sure to be incorporating it into your each day.

The next maximum crucial concept is that of making the moment the great it may be, via following the IMPROVE acronym. This acronym is wonderful used with a purpose to improve the outstanding of moments which is probably especially tough for you. Remember to make as superb of use of this as you can even as you want to, and don't be afraid to put in writing those gadgets on study gambling cards with the intention to bear in mind them.

The first of those thoughts is imagery. Imagery is ready placing your self in every different location mentally. When matters get especially distressing, don't be afraid to remember some issue that isn't distressing. Imagine your preferred vicinity, what it'd be like if topics were going the manner you favored them to, or simply normally a few issue that makes you satisfied like your domestic dog or your kids. Putting yourself a few different location to your thoughts can be very powerful in making you enjoy which include you're higher equipped to cope with the state of affairs to hand through permitting you to relax.

The next idea is which means. Try to are attempting to find out an great motive for the emotion you're experiencing. In essence, in case you're feeling a certain way, in preference to rejecting your emotions subconsciously, permit your self to don't forget why you're feeling the way that you are and what motive it serves.

After that comes prayer. Do look at that prayer doesn't constantly should be spiritual in nature. There are plenty of studies that have confirmed that smooth recitation of a few element calming has the equal subconscious rest effects as prayer does. The detail that you're in reality taking benefit of is liberating steam and finding tranquility in some element, whether or not or not or now not it is a word or a deity. In that, in case you don't mainly worship any person you could pray to, offer you with a personal mantra you could say if you want to make your self sense higher. If you do have someone you pray to, then take the possibility to talk to them approximately your situation; it will make you revel in such as you're greater able to take delivery of and deal with it.

Next inside the decorate set comes relaxation. Relaxation is precisely what it seems like. Take the risk to simply loosen up your muscle agencies and use a number of your self-soothing strategies so you can become generally calmer and further prepared to in reality obtain the given second. Also, allow's be sincere: at the same time as you're annoying and feeling typically out of it, you're now not going to be at your outstanding in phrases of rationality. You have to be staying as cushty as possible generally to be able to make sure which you aren't going to have an irrational response to 3 aspect.

After that comes one. This is ready being able to interest on a unique element. We keep coming decrease lower back so far as it's important to pressure the functionality to keep yourself transferring second to 2nd and now not get stuck up in matters that you can't always control. This will will let you stay centered, not lose your train of idea, and preserve to assess subjects as they will be. In combination at the aspect of your mindfulness education to check subjects in a nonjudgmental way, this really turns into one of the maximum powerful gear in your arsenal. You'll slowly advantage the potential to take a look at topics thru a much more healthy lens than you can in advance than.

Next comes vacation. Vacation is all approximately letting your self take a damage from some component you're doing, probable even a actual vacation.

Keep it brief, even though, otherwise you'll lose steam. However, it's very annoying in your mind to attempt to maintain it in check all the time. Don't allow it interest on something is stressing you out; allow it drift from trouble remember to trouble rely in a carefree way at the same time as you permit the world round you skip you thru for a hint bit.

Last, and this is most really no longer least - in fact, it's one of the maximum essential things inside the ebook that we haven't quite covered but - is encouraging your self. This is a important expertise to boom in dealing with inconsistent feelings and irregular reactions. The fact is that in case you are having to look at this the least bit, you experience to three diploma which consist of you aren't completely able to deal with some of the subjects that display up in lifestyles. This can be because of early trauma, genetics, your surroundings growing up, your cutting-edge-day surroundings, or any combination of things sincerely. This manner in the long run which you constantly have a voice internal your head telling you that you may't do it.

I'm going to digress for a 2d, to be actual and honest with you. The fact is that maximum people who exercise dialectical behavior remedy achieve this due to the fact they have borderline character illness. When people have borderline personality sickness, their diagnosis isn't precisely incredible. While it's in massive element treatable with appropriate enough remedy and probable supplemental treatment to useful useful resource with depression, ten percent of humans with borderline personality illness will become killing themselves. This is a sad and terrifying huge range.

If you are reading this because you've got borderline individual illness, otherwise you take a look at about it and assume that you could in shape the invoice, I'd need to refer you to looking for the help of a medical professional who can be there in individual with you and communicate you via the numerous one-of-a-type options. Depression is actual, it's miles heavy, and borderline persona illness is constantly comorbid with it. While each person can revel in the talents which can be advanced via dialectical behavior remedy, in case you're right right here due to the fact you fear that you can have borderline individual disorder, looking for correct help and get right into a application with a personal therapist so you'll be sure you're getting the wonderful and most customized revel in possible.

The motive that that is applicable and no longer a whole digression is that once in a while, the capability to inspire your self is going to be very, very tough to keep. In truth, if you do have depression comorbid collectively together with your temper or character sickness, the possibilities are excellent that when I say you need to cheer your self on, you haven't any idea what I'm even speaking about. While it's clean to mention from a certain attitude that you preferably ought to inform your self that you could perform a little issue, it's no longer the fact of the situation that absolutely because of the truth you do it, you're going to consider it.

At first, whilst you tell yourself that you may do it, you're in all likelihood not even going to have an emotional kickback reaction; you're going to invite yourself, "what if I can't? Why must I be capable of do it?" and that may be a sad region to begin. But even in case you don't take delivery of as right with it, you need to faux it till you're making it.

There are an entire lot of motives that that is commonly useful. Your thoughts accepts what it's given in the end, and if you say that you can carry out a bit element, it's going to through the years be given as actual with that it could. What you are announcing and do is a very effective emotional input, and latest mental studies have set up that faking it till you are making it's miles a very actual phenomenon in phrases of your thoughts structure.

More than that, the very act of telling yourself that you may do it, and take transport of whatever is going on, and address it properly, is incredibly powerful. It's a mental sword, if you'll. If you try this, you can assemble the talent to accept what is coming your way and certainly paintings your manner via it all, no matter what it is able to be. Telling yourself that you can do it is impactful.

Beyond all of that, through the years you're going to amplify the ability to simply accept as proper with yourself, due to the truth the clean truth that you are going to make it through the whole thing which you're seeking to do. While you may no longer be given as actual with it, you may typically be able to ultimately address a few issue you're looking to do. Think of it this manner: all of life follows the identical sample. They are each shifting in advance, or they're at rock bottom, and rock backside implicates loss of life. If you aren't death, you then're progressing nonetheless. Find safety in that reality. Your thoughts is designed to deal with severa topics, even though it couldn't be designed to deal with them proper now. Your mind particularly has a tough time with this, due to the reality for one purpose or every different your mind has end up burdened to cope with things in an risky way.

However, that doesn't imply you can't undo this, and extra importantly, the issue of all of that is that tough matters are, properly, difficult. You're going to need to artwork to get thru them, and lamentably that's clearly the character of the beast. However, if you go through that during thoughts and ultimately paintings on accepting that truth, then you definately definately definately'll start to apprehend with time that at the identical time as you tell yourself you can cope with some issue, which you in the end do. This will enhance the declaration.

The declaration moreover serves to make you extra resilient to some thing may moreover appear to you. For example, in case you tell your self that you can deal with things constantly, if matters do worsen or if every other terrible trouble does seem, you'll bear in mind which you're able to address them every time they do come up. Ultimately, you'll preserve in thoughts that the electricity absolutely lies internal you to make what desires to arise, arise. This is your exceptional device - your ability to inspire yourself and maintain in thoughts that some thing it takes, you can do it.

That brings an give up to the specific decorate set. As I said earlier, try to discover a manner to artwork those into your every day regular on the equal time as you're doing the distress tolerance block so that you can don't forget them better while the time comes. Also take into account placing them up in this type of manner that you may see them whenever you most find out yourself desiring them. This may be some thing as clean as writing them down in a notes app in your telephone and summarizing them surely so that they're interior smooth reach, or perhaps taking a screenshot of the pages that they're written on in case you're studying this on a few issue like a Kindle or Books app.

The subsequent big part of misery tolerance is the functionality to evaluate the professionals and cons of a few component. Think approximately your given situation and remember what positives and negatives can come from it if you make a decision no longer to tolerate the situation. Is there any actual and proactive change that you may provoke?

A lot of the time, whilst you're attempting actively now not to do a little issue, there can be a kickback response on your mind so that it will show up till you respond to it. (Unless you have got have been given OCD, in which case that is most probably a compulsion and also you need to avoid meditating on it.) Until you satisfy the answer of what ought to take area in case you did respond to a state of affairs - and study such in a realistic manner - you aren't going to experience snug with now not responding to the state of affairs. This shouldn't arise all the time, as it's a terrible dependancy to ingrain, however when you do have the kickback response it's now not a lousy issue to think objectively approximately what may and wouldn't happen if you did determine to reply to the given stimulus.

Another element that you need to exercise is the idea of standard popularity. The fact is that numerous the time, you're seeking to actively fight in opposition to the truth of a scenario. Sometimes, that is due to the truth you sense like you may't control it. Other instances, it's due to the truth you don't want to lapse control of the scenario. In those kinds of situations, what you ultimately want to do is allow yourself to absolutely and average receive some thing is taking region to you.

The fact is that you aren't going to change a fact that you could't alternate, regardless of how an lousy lot you try. Focusing in your disability to trade it will handiest prove stressful. There are some subjects which you excellent have a lot of a hand in. In these cases, you may wonderful do as heaps as you are able to do, and no amount of your movement will alternate it.

Consider, as an example, an illness inside the family. What need to you in reality do to trade this disturbing state of affairs?

Can you take away their infection? Can you fight closer to this tide? No, lamentably. The sad reality is which you can't. And even because it's painful, the first-rate problem that you may do that is wholesome is to accept something may additionally appear as some thing which you aren't able to change.

This ought to be practiced in tandem collectively with your mindfulness strategies and your self-discipline such which you're able to exercise the subsequent potential: turning your mind. The goal of this abilities is strolling to your capacity to make yourself take shipping of what is taking vicinity in preference to rejecting it. One of the essential troubles in issues like borderline man or woman disease is that you increase a character which of its very nature has a completely difficult time accepting some element is taking place. Your knee-jerk reaction is to reject some element is taking area because it technique lapsing manipulate of the situation or being powerless.

You need to paintings on honing that capability so you can start to receive some thing may also take location. You want to exercising your potential to make yourself accept topics. Acceptance is a addiction, and even as you shouldn't take transport of the entirety which passes, you need to learn how to take delivery of those topics which you have no hand in. Any different reaction is irrational, as there was little that you can have finished to alternate it. While you can combat with yourself over what this phrase simply approach and whether or no longer or no longer or no longer you could do something to alternate some thing, the best answer is the right one: often, you could't.

Building the dependancy of reputation will shift you closer to a commonly greater wholesome kingdom of mind if you want to can help you start to paintings with topics and mind in a miles better way than you're proper now. You'll be able to gadget your feelings in a higher way.

All of those skills culminate within the final potential of misery tolerance that is to examine the difference among being inclined to do some component and being excessively willful. Willingness is the need to do this that could genuinely have an impact. For instance, if you don't like how masses you are making and you could financially manage to pay for to move and get a few other degree, you need to be inclined to get a diploma. Don't be given a terrible lot in life really due to the fact you boom an reputation stance. Willfulness is the choice to perform a touch factor that may't have an effect; in essence, willfulness is being excessively willful to the element that you need to alternate topics that you can not. In those cases, your willfulness is breaking from your potential to be accepting of the things you can't trade, which reasons needless internal anxiety. You need to release that anxiety and allow yourself to accept that that you can't trade. In that, you could discover your area in lifestyles turning into happier and your manner of looking at life becoming more healthy. You will now not obsess over changing things you can't, but you may discover your self being greater inclined to do the ones subjects which is probably powerful.

That all brings the financial ruin on distress tolerance to the quit. All of these competencies have to be practiced at some point of your misery tolerance block. There have been severa acronyms that you had to workout and keep, so try to get to paintings on doing that so you can do not forget the ones in your every day lifestyles.

The essential component to examine approximately your blocks, if you haven't already, is that you want to be carrying those competencies into your every day lifestyles even out of doors in their precise block; the ideal block is simply intended to offer you a time for prolonged attention on a given situation so you can train the ones techniques and start going for walks on maintaining them.

If you're studying via this book proper away and thinking that you need to try to implement all of those items straight away, I'd want to offer you with a warning not to; your remedy may be extra vain. Your thoughts isn't set up to address that loads trade right away. Remember that that could be a marathon and now not a sprint, similar to I said earlier; your achievement with those techniques is in particular hooked up upon your ability to preserve these things and use them actionably. Carry them with you, but don't load they all on your self straight away.

Chapter 5: Building Your Emotional Regulation

At this factor in the sport, we reach the second one to ultimate most essential capability which you're in search of to teach via those dialectical behavior treatment techniques. This is emotional law.

Note that all of these skills intertwine with every one of a kind in a very essential way. Mindfulness, as an instance, offers you the capability to address misery tolerance and emotional law with the detachment that they deserve; misery tolerance offers you an critical base for regulating your feelings even as instances get in particular difficult; and emotional law builds on mindfulness competencies and misery tolerance talents so one can will allow you to regulate your emotions to the finest quantity feasible. Interpersonal effectiveness is ready operating for your potential to make your conversations with others extra effective in connection with the topics we've already referred to.

So, what is emotional regulation, and what is the purpose in the back of it? Well, to reply the primary question, emotional regulation is notably self-explanatory. It's a hard and fast of diverse approaches and systems that have been superior if you want to assist humans who have issues controlling their feelings in a extra regular, ordinary, and healthful way.

Ultimately, it's simply the concept of metering your terrible and dangerous emotions on this kind of way that you could turn out to be a better man or woman all round and address severa one-of-a-kind troubles in a greater conducive way. It moreover lets in you to construct a better sense of detachment and attractiveness out of your problems so you can higher isolate their root reasons and determine out what you could be doing that allows you to better assist yourself.

This is crucial to people who are suffering from such things as borderline individual illness or who are suicidal or in any other case emotionally volatile because of the fact they have a tendency to have unpredictable and excessive emotions; as an example, you will possibly feel irritated, depressed, annoying, or inexplicably indignant. While this stuff are suitable and understandable feelings in an entire lot of distinct times - honestly blocking off out your feelings is without a doubt as terrible as having too excessive of emotions - you need to learn how to revel in them at an emotionally healthy stage and no longer allow them to become ordinary or irrational.

The first capability that you want to do at the way to adjust your emotions is to understand what feelings you're feeling and why you're feeling them. You can try this by the usage of manner of breaking them down with what's called the tale of emotion.

The tale of emotion is a essential skill in breaking down your emotions and records what precisely it is that you're feeling. Some feelings are mainly hard to manner, and you don't constantly revel in in reality one emotion; frequently, you'll sense multiple straight away in a totally disconnected kind of manner. What do you do in this shape of state of affairs? Well, you damage down multiple signs and reflect onconsideration on what they will suggest which you're feeling.

The first factor you want to investigate is what precisely prompted what you're feeling. This may be a large tell in some problem emotion you're experiencing. If a person cuts within the the the front of you in net web site site visitors, you may possibly have purpose to experience angry, for example.

The 2nd problem you need to research is the manner you interpreted the occasion. What took place for your eyes, how did you are taking it in? What are you able to do on the way to distance your self from the event a bit bit and study it with alternatively clearer eyes? All of this may have a massive impact for your response.

The 1/3 detail you want to investigate is what you're feeling in terms of your body. Do you've got a pit of fireplace to your stomach? Does it sense like your belly is churning? Our thoughts has all sorts of interesting strategies of indicating to us that we're feeling a certain way about a few component. It's a very interesting shape of intertwining phenomenon among our thoughts and our frame.

The fourth detail you have got got to research is the way you're subconsciously reacting to the occasion. Are your palms crossed? Do you experience greater emotionally closed off than you probably did preceding to the occasion? Is your jaw or face demanding, or are your eyes wider than everyday? All of these styles of subjects imply unique emotions.

The fifth detail that you have to investigate is what you experience the urge to do. If you experience the urge to ram into the decrease again of a person's car when they lessen you off, the risk is right which you're feeling anger, as an instance. You can recognize your feelings primarily based off of the element that they make you want to do.

The 6th issue that you need to understand is the movement which you took. Did you curse after they reduce you off, or flip them off? This is however another indicator that you are indignant. These sorts of matters permit you to know what you're feeling.

The very last problem you want to research is the call of the emotion, deliberating all the exclusive subjects on the listing. If you're feeling irritated, apprehend which you're feeling indignant based totally off of the truth that you did angry subjects and had what you perceived as a purpose to be angry.

There's a exceptional amount of significance in all of this; at the same time as it can seem stupid to tell yourself what you're feeling, it could be a extraordinary tool for placing matters into attitude and analyzing what you're feeling underneath the hood. It also can make you realize which you're feeling irrationally about some issue and that you need to take a step yet again if in any respect possible. Recognizing what you're feeling can do hundreds in phrases of metering what you're feeling.

The very last reason is to distance your self from what is called the "emotion thoughts"; in doing this, you gather your capability to apprehend and adapt to subjects together together with your conscious and conscious mind in preference to reacting in a visceral and nearly primal manner based absolutely off of some element your wit and whimsy may be.

There are some of of factors that you could do in terms of your bodily health at the manner to allow you higher adjust your feelings. You can don't forget those via the acronym PLEASE.

The first detail within the PLEASE set is Physical fitness. Pay near interest in your bodily fitness; if you are sick or harm in a few type of manner, you need to do what you can to get to a health practitioner and get it taken care of. When you're ill, you don't have as lots energy as you generally should to hold control of your mind.

The 2nd factor inside the set is proper Eating conduct. This is prepared reviewing the manner in that you consume and ensuring that you're getting all of the vitamins that you need. Don't devour an excessive amount of or too little and eat right meals if in any respect feasible in location of junk meals. Sometimes, budget get inside the way of this; don't make the mistake of questioning that reasonably-priced meals can't be healthy food, despite the reality that. Things at the side of canned carrots and spinach, beans, rice, and so on are all healthful staple meals that may be prepared in severa tremendous strategies and that percentage a ton of nutrients.

The 1/three issue is avoidance of medicine. Essentially, drop all matters that you could which modify your temper. This is mostly a big deal for folks that suffer from such things as borderline person disease due to the fact they have a propensity to have high prices of substance abuse as properly. This isn't me trying to be D.A.R.E., that could be a proper concept; capsules might also moreover make you revel in better inside the quick time, but they have got an not unusual unpredictable impact on your lengthy-term mood. Some humans locate remedy in positive subjects which may be prescribed, and that's o.K.. The scenario is extra with things like alcohol, opiates, and stimulants. Things of this nature can reason your moods to be unpredictable and greater volatile than traditional, especially because of their addictive functionality.

The fourth factor is napping behavior. Be certain which you're getting the proper amount of sleep. Try to get among seven and nine hours in keeping with night time time. More or plenty a great deal much less can throw your frame's chemistry out of whack in quite fundamental tactics, on the way to destroy your temper commonly.

The very last factor is exercising. Exercise is a cornerstone of every intellectual and bodily fitness. In terms of physical health, you'll experience together with you look better in case you do a right quantity of exercise. In terms of intellectual health, exercise motives the release of endorphins and diverse chemical substances for your thoughts which purpose you to experience better and happier in stylish.

That brings an end to the PLEASE set. In addition to the PLEASE set, you need to art work on constructing self-control through strolling on as a minimum one detail each day. Try to come to be mastering some aspect. This will make you feel better about your self and train you masses approximately strength of will and self-control in addition to creating you sense commonly more capable.

A big cornerstone of this specific block of dialectical behavior remedy is which you are capable of efficiently use the idea of contrary motion. Opposite movement is used so you can scale back your urges and do and experience the "proper" detail if you have an emotion it's difficult to justify.

Through emotional reflected image and detachment, you need that allows you to understand at the same time as it's right or incorrect to enjoy an emotion. If you sense some thing that you ideally shouldn't be feeling, use opposite movement.

Opposite movement is the idea which you do some aspect is the complete opposite of the urges that you're having in that given moment. This is used for volatile and self-destructive feelings like unjustified anger or annoyance. Instead of doing whatever the emotion makes you experience specifically pressured to do in that second, do something is the polar contrary of that.

This in impact reasons you to leave the emotion you aren't searching behind with the useful useful resource of alternatively feeling the emotion it simply is the exact opposite. While this does come upon as a piece reductionist, using it is in reality as a substitute intuitive and also you'll in all likelihood discover that it permit you to to feel hundreds higher in emotionally unstable conditions.

So, what if your emotion is justified? What are you capable of do? This is the capability of problem fixing. Detach your self from the scenario and word what you realistically are able to do as a manner to remedy it. If you can't do some factor, then be given the state of affairs available and permit your self to feel the emotion. If you can carry out a touch difficulty, then take low priced, actionable, and powerful steps ahead so you can begin ameliorating the scenario this is troubling you.

The last key concept of emotional regulation goes hand in hand with the popularity and mindfulness subjects that we've referred to already. This is letting float of your feelings. The concept, as I said earlier, isn't to block out your feelings absolutely however alternatively to experience them in a rational and comparatively healthy manner.

Think approximately the emotion that you're feeling; deliver it authentic notion and take transport of that whatever it's miles, it's going on. Acceptance of an emotion does not generally suggest response to it; it in reality approach which you famend that the emotion is taking area. Once you've completed so, you may truly permit the emotion pass over you.

Using all of these skills together, you have got a terrific base for emotional law. Remember, you're seeking to make yourself happier and construct a lifestyles properly worth dwelling. You can fantastic do that by way of studying to have problem in terms of your every day emotions and letting your self sense in a healthy manner.

Chapter 6: Interpersonal Effectiveness

The final unique functionality that you're seeking to construct through dialectical behavior remedy is interpersonal effectiveness. Interpersonal effectiveness is used with a purpose to let you assert your self effectively, deal with warfare, and address human beings in a well mannered and empathetic way.

The hassle for lots people with dialectical behavior treatment is they discover it tough to apply their commonly suitable interpersonal capabilities to a communique that they're actively having.

The first component which you want to workout with is your capacity to supply your emotions and desires to someone else. This is all supposed that will help you efficiently get what you need whenever you do want a few issue. You can do is the use of the acronym DEEAR MAN.

D stands for describe, regarding you describing the state of affairs which you're in as objectively and nonjudgmentally as viable, the usage of your mindfulness skills to detach from it.

E stands for unique, regarding your capability to inform them the manner you felt whilst the scenario occurred, what reasons this to be an problem for you, and the manner you currently experience concerning the state of affairs.

The 2nd E stands for empathy; bear in mind what they're feeling and what they've experienced. This is vital in growing an equal emotional playing vicinity and being capable of ask for some aspect it's miles which you're requesting.

A stands for assert, regarding your ability to precise what you need in a completely easy and unique way.

R stands for make more potent; offer a superb reinforcement inside the event that they ought to do what you're searching them to do.

M stands for aware; continue to be as privy to the scenario as possible, staying centered on the element which you want and transferring the verbal exchange once more to that pertinent topic if the alternative man or woman actions some distance from it.

A stands for seem, regarding the way you venture yourself. Project self guarantee even though you may not surely be confident.

N stands for negotiate, relating to the truth that if someone is hesitant, come to a compromise with them after putting forward your self sincerely so that you may be on the identical page.

Using the ones abilties, you may be capable of greater assertively and correctly ask anyone for some issue; this expertise could be very critical in growing your functionality to be greater demanding and get up for your self.

The second set of talents is intended that will help you with retaining your relationships and make human beings experience open towards you. They are essentially to help you radiate warm temperature and regular be a more enjoyable man or woman to be spherical. They may be remembered the usage of the acronym GIVE.

The first letter, G, refers to gentleness: be slight with the man or woman in query, don't be judgmental, general simply be a first rate man or woman using language which is wholesome for the state of affairs. Don't reduce the character down and usually be courteous. Good-natured joking could be very properly so long as the alternative individual is k with it, and sarcasm should be averted till they've made it clean that they're ok with it.

The second letter, I, refers to hobby: show the person that you're inquisitive about acting involved. Don't push back your eyes, ask them questions each time the immediately is proper, and avoid having any distractions out that can make it look like you don't care approximately what they have to say.

The 0.33 letter, V, refers to validation: display which you recognize what they're attempting to mention and what they're searching to speak. Demonstrate that you can sympathize with them. You don't necessarily have to mention it; you may unique it via your frame language and the manner which you react facially.

The fourth letter, E, refers to easiness: have an easy disposition. Be as calm and comfortable as you can be, lead them to snigger, and keep in mind to illustrate which you're snug thru smiling and now not seeming along with you're dire all the time.

Through the usage of those unique guidelines, you'll assemble an crucial repertoire for making your self come off as annoying, empathetic, and warmth. This will foster relationships with people no matter who they will be and make you come off as an amazing individual to realise and be round.

The final acronym, FAST, is primarily based around your functionality to hold your feature and understand your rate, not losing your feel of self-respect for everyone. This is significantly important, due to the fact humans with borderline person disease normally have a tendency to make investments an excessive amount of of themselves into all and sundry else's opinion and could often trade themselves for them. You can gather your revel in of self-recognize and your opinion of your self by means of sticking to it.

The f stands for straightforward: normally be honest, every to yourself and to the individual that you're speakme to.

The a stands for apologizing: do apologize, however no longer an excessive amount of. You don't have any purpose to make an apology more than as speedy as for a few aspect which you've done ineffectively. You shouldn't experience which includes you do.

The s stands for staying: live right for your beliefs and your values. Don't let humans tell you that you ought to be a few issue aside from you are or experience a few aspect aside from you revel in. This doesn't recommend which you want to bullheadedly reject something that a person tells you; you need to maintain an open mind, of direction, and inside the event that they have specific purpose to say you're incorrect then undergo in mind the possibility that you may be. However, within the event that they're in reality being advocate or trying to get you to carry out a touch element you generally wouldn't, admire yourself enough to paste on your guns.

The t stands for reality: in no way lie. Lies simplest assemble upon themselves, harm your relationships, and in the long run culminate in the damaging of your very own feel of self-recognize as nicely.

These are, in essence, the belongings you want to workout and maintain in thoughts at some point of your interpersonal effectiveness block. Carry them with you in a while as you improvement in addition.

That brings an quit to the precise competencies that you want to exercise as a way to genuinely get the blessings of dialectical conduct remedy. If you pay close to interest to them and try to observe the values, then you can come out the opportunity give up a stronger and happier person. The give up reason is to assemble a existence surely well worth dwelling, and I anticipate that you could do it.

Chapter 7: Helping Somebody Else

This financial disaster goes to focus on the topics that you could do in case you need to help any character else who is trying to do dialectical behavior treatment.

The first factor which you need to recognize is which you need to try and get them to go to a actual therapist if feasible. You may be type and compassionate, however you are not professional. You cannot do all of this on your personal, and you aren't always certified to do dialectical behavior treatment. If you do attempt, even though, there are some of of factors which you need to maintain in mind.

The first is that a crux of dialectical conduct treatment as a therapist discern is that you validate their feelings, however tell them once they're doing some thing that's vain, useless meaning a few issue it clearly is self-destructive or potentially dangerous to them.

You additionally need to guide them to sense like they may be as open as viable. Another motive that therapists can frequently be advanced is that they have impartiality. While they do charge cash, that money comes with a promise of revel in, confidentiality, and qualification. Be as warmth and receptive to them, however don't red meat up terrible behaviors.

Ensure that they stay on target. Keep a document for them of the subjects that they try this inhibit their personal improvement in advance, like failing to maintain a right meditation habitual. Go over this with them as soon as every week and reason them to aware about the topics they're doing ineffectively. Gently remind them that they aren't going to make development within the event that they don't make try.

In essence, the brilliant element that you may do to assist someone else is to redirect them to all of us who is licensed to assist. Understandably, despite the fact that, every now and then that isn't an desire. In this case, make yourself as warm temperature and receptive to them as possible, permit them to be open, perform a little component you could to make certain they keep respecting you - they manifestly do, or they wouldn't ask you to assist them with such sincerity in the first region.

It's an prolonged and tough journey, and you want to anticipate on the manner to pick up the cellphone in the event that they need steerage at any factor for at least six months. If you could do this, be accepting, be warmth, and be unbiased and aim, then you may maybe assist them.

Chapter 8: Dialectical Behavior Therapy For Teens

Some teens conflict with normal lifestyles. For a younger individual who feels unprepared, careworn or unworthy, the sector can be a scary region.

This is in which DBT can make a distinction. Teens can get preserve of peer help and robust guidance to sense better about themselves.

Dialectical conduct treatment, or DBT treatment, efficaciously allows adjust and accurate tough, unproductive, or perhaps self-unfavorable idea styles. Behaviors and emotions which could negatively impact a teen's existence are examined, explored, and dealt with with compassion and in a manner to empower them.

DBT treatment gives younger humans with concrete and identifiable capabilities and encouragement that builds don't forget and competence. Teens regularly find that it encourages self-reputation and healthy, proactive desire-making competencies.

They discover ways to examine and manage change, pressure and unpredictability— vital existence abilties that increase a teen's intellectual flexibility and sensible capability to address difficult times.

Most of what we take a look at these days is about getting your baby to clean their room or be extra accountable, the manner to address rebellious, defiant, out of manage and competitive teenagers—but little has been written about this from the teen's thing of view.

It made me count on that nowadays, we need to examine the trouble in any other case. I took a extraordinary have a examine my boys, accompanied them, chatted to them a bit, talked to unique young adults, and that's what I determined.

THE MOST COMMON PROBLEMS TEENAGERS FACE TODAY

Teenagers aged 13-19 face real issues on a each day foundation as this is the maximum tough boom section in their existence. During this time, teens are exposed to overwhelming outdoor and internal struggles. They cope with hormonal modifications, puberty, social and parental forces, paintings and university pressures, and lots of others. Many young adults experience misunderstood. It is vital that their thoughts and emotions are proven and that validation comes from their dad and mom. Parents ought to speak to their young adults thoughtfully and lightly whilst discussing their troubles and issues.

The common problems that teens face in recent times relate to:

1. Body photograph troubles

Your body image is what you trust you studied and feel approximately your body. This includes the manner you see your non-public body, which may also or may not in form the form and length of your frame.

A first-class or healthful frame photograph manner feeling satisfied and satisfied collectively together with your frame and look. Conversely, an awful or terrible frame picture way being upset at the side of your appearance. People who experience this frequently want to alternate the dimensions or form of their our our our bodies.

A teen's risky body image is right now related to low conceitedness, critical to negative moods and mood swings.

Young individuals who sense depressed are much more likely to pay hobby at the lousy messages spherical them and have interaction in negative comparisons among their our our bodies and what they see as an "satisfactory" frame. Poor frame image and occasional arrogance are danger elements for growing volatile weight loss behaviors, consuming problems, and intellectual problems which encompass depression.

2. Community and identity goals which may be unmet

When young adults get the message that they don't belong and don't healthy in, this may reason feelings of disconnection, isolation and depression.

Teens want to enjoy a part of a network, but many teenagers find it hard to be regular.

three. Time control pressure

Stress will boom at college and with age— the big kind of duties to be completed, trials to be faced, no longer to mention sports activities activities and different extracurricular sports. A new attractive horizon opens up at the social stage: conferences, events, and outings with pals. In addition, they're continuously distracted with the useful resource of digital media in the path of this time. A teen who tries to satisfy a number of these expectations becomes compelled.

4. Social and parental stress

Parents often stay through their youngsters and count on them to acquire the whole thing they desired to but didn't. Expecting your little one to have real grades, have proper friends, excel at extracurricular activities, carry out nicely, be accountable for himself and now and again his greater younger brothers and sisters is lots of strain. Added to that is peer stress. In order to be diagnosed thru the usage of their peers and grow to be "well-known," teens experience pressured to conform to their tastes, behaviors and appears.

five. Mental and physical fitness troubles

Some factors terrible to a youngster's health encompass:

• Bad vitamins. Adolescents' consuming conduct are regularly horrible and out of manage. They usually have a tendency towards eating troubles, each starving or gorging on unhealthy, fatty, and excessive-calorie junk food.

• Lack of sleep. In an attempt to do the whole lot and be the entirety, teenagers sacrifice sleep. They need about nine hours of sleep, however teens get approximately seven hours of sleep on common. This manner that they're in deficit every day.

• Depression and anxiety. Adding to the chaos and strain of normal living, hormonal shifts positioned teenagers underneath large emotional stress. This is contemplated in tension, mood swings, aggression, melancholy and sometimes even a whole breakdown.

Mental health and bodily health are related. If your little one isn't always in right physical fitness, it's going to have an effect on his psychology and vice versa.

6. Lack of wonderful heroes and feature models

The wealthiest spoilt brats, biggest bullies, and maximum adverse children are frequently considered the maximum right and well-known. The media glorify those human beings, and awful behavior is applauded in movies, sports sports and song. Wherever they pass, our kids are fed a weight loss program of terrible role fashions and function absorbed the depraved values of the "heroes" portrayed inside the media.

7. Drugs and alcohol

Alcohol and marijuana can harm a teen's developing brain. Talking to them can be very important to find out what's taking place in university and with their peer institution; discover what they're exposed to and train your infant approximately the dangers round them.

8. Unhealthy social media and on-display violence

When used responsibly, Twitter, Facebook, Instagram, and specific social systems can be outstanding techniques for teens to connect with the arena; however, they will be tough while applied in a risky manner. Violent video video games promote violence and aggression. Going online exposes teens to evil characters, lousy humans, risky pics, pornography, violence, and sexual content cloth. Regardless of what you do or try to do, there's no manner to absolutely shield them. It is as a good deal as parents to recognize what their youngsters are doing on-line and train them the way to engage thoroughly on the internet.

9. Intimidation

Many are unaware that bullying may be direct or indirect; this consists of rumor-mongering and gossip. Many youngsters don't even recognize what cyberbullying is or don't absolutely understand the likely risky consequences in their online conduct.

10. Sexual hobby and risky behaviors

Research constantly suggests that most parents don't suppose their youngsters are sexually active. Again, speakme approximately intercourse in conjunction with your children is crucial, even if you don't anticipate they will be having sex.

The troubles above are because of low arrogance and an loss of capability to manipulate and manage emotions. DBT can assist.

THE BIOLOGICAL AND ENVIRONMENTAL FACTORS BEHIND MOOD SWINGS IN TEENAGERS

Researchers have first-rate information if you're the decide of a youngster laid low with extreme temper swings. These feelings are normal and want to subside as your little one progresses into childhood.

But if the stormy emotional seas don't subside as teenagers method maturity, it may be a warning to dad and mom of greater intense issues.

Research shows that teenage temper swings are extra volatile in early young adults and have a propensity to stabilize as teenagers emerge as vintage. In early youth, cognitive manage structures lag in the back of emotional improvement, making it difficult for teens to address their feelings.

Apart from biological factors, many changes rise up in some unspecified time in the future of formative years, collectively with moving into immoderate university, quarreling with mother and father, and the reports of past love and breakups.

Research indicates that as teens grow to be older, they advantage greater control over their emotions, conflicts with dad and mom will lower, and that they normally discover ways to manage their moods higher.

WHAT CAN PARENTS DO TO HELP TEENAGERS

Adolescence can be a hard time of trade for dad and mom and young adults. But on the same time as the ones years may be difficult, there is a lot you may do to take care of your toddler and inspire responsible behavior. Develop parenting competencies for raising a teenager. Here are a few sports to assist your young adults:

• We cannot forget about our parental responsibilities. Even regardless of the fact that they are young adults, they however want us, just like once they have been small. But, cell phones, laptop systems and one in all a type devices can not offer the care they want.

• Create lines of conversation which might be so robust that your youngsters will normally see you as allies in desire to enemies. Communicate positively and keep away from instructions.

• We want to find out techniques to help teenagers, make bigger our parenting capabilities, save you complaining and take obligation for our teenagers now.

• Offer healthy and healthy meals, along with fruit and veggies.

• Discuss and set up guidelines for residence duties, homework, riding, dating, sex, and drug and alcohol use. Keep talking about most of those troubles.

• Let them recognise that you don't usually have all the answers and aren't continuously proper. Listen to their views and provide help while desired.

• Be prepared to concentrate their issue of view. Think cautiously in advance than throwing their mind in the trash. An mind-set of encouragement and guide is going a protracted manner.

• Look for signs and symptoms and signs and signs and symptoms of pressure, anxiety, lack of interest, horrible ingesting conduct, terrible private and oral hygiene, sleep disturbances, and decreased hobby in social sports and cope with them right now.

• Punishing teens doesn't really paintings, however disciplining them does. So ensure your rules help instead of damage.

• Be type sufficient to thank them, recognize them, and love them on every occasion viable.

• Fear of failure is a fantastic motive of stress, so help them manage their anxiety and construct their self-esteem.

• If your teenager suggests symptoms and signs and signs and symptoms of melancholy or anxiety, get assist proper away.

• Above all, allow them to recognize you care!

The most treasured component parents can do for his or her teen kids is establish particular verbal exchange.

A easy conversation channel opens up many opportunities. This improves the relationship and permits the child take delivery of as actual with the dad and mom on touchy issues alongside aspect bullying, peer pressure, and abuse. As cited in advance, dad and mom must sense snug speakme to their youngsters about a few commonplace teenage troubles, collectively with relationship, intercourse, capsules, and alcohol. This incapacity to speak about top and evil leads them to take the wrong steps out of interest. Effective verbal exchange will sell keep in mind, admire and recognition among the adolescent and mother and father.

There are severa benefits to often sharing your thoughts and thoughts collectively together with your children and giving them the danger to precise their critiques. Here are a number of them:

Improve their verbal abilities

Speaking regularly collectively together along with your toddler will make sure that they continuously beautify their vocabulary, and modeling their parents can advocate that they'll enhance their records of sentence form. In addition, if youngsters regularly particular their views to mother and father, they may beautify their presentation talents in beauty.

Improve emotional literacy

Children who can not specific what they may be feeling may also moreover revel in annoyed and take it out on others in a few unspecified time inside the future. On the alternative hand, if children can virtually articulate their feelings, they'll be more likely to solve their troubles through speak in place of in other techniques.

Understanding your son or daughter

Talking for your youngsters to percent their hopes, dreams, and fears approach you can understand your toddler higher. While many parents lead busy lives, taking time to talk with their kids at the college run or spherical a table technique they experience listened to and liked.

Understanding instructions

Children commonly collect guidance at home and school, which may be overwhelming at instances. Communicating quick, direct commands at regular periods can be a good deal much less tough for youngsters to digest, at the identical time as everyday communique way they may query some thing they don't understand.

Monitoring your child's improvement

As children pass essential milestones, their workloads and capabilities trade. Talking approximately kids's dreams, homework plans, and examination results advocate that parents have a splendid idea in their children's progress.

Behavior in college

At college, teens are predicted to interact with their friends, instructors, and unique body of employees in a well mannered manner and politely. Exercising those talents in ordinary communique together with your kids will help you put corporation limitations for their behavior.

FIVE SKILLS NECESSARY TO BE A PARENT OF AN EMOTIONAL TEENAGER

Anyone can emerge as a parent; however, you want to take a look at some parenting talents and increase right abilties to be a awesome discern for your emotional teen.

You can only assist your teenager control their feelings in case you recognize how to attend to yours.

Parents need to investigate 5 talent gadgets to attain success in raising an emotional or excessive-threat teenager:

Mindfulness abilties

Mindfulness is a manner that could reduce parental pressure. Mindfulness is a manner of being. Practicing mindfulness way paying attention to what is taking location proper now and accepting the ones studies and emotions without judgment. So how does it art work within the every day lifestyles of a determine?

Here are 5 processes to live conscious for the day.

• Accept your infant (and your self) without judgment
• Listen cautiously for your child
• Imagine your toddler's feelings and react as a consequence
• Show compassion for your self and your infant
• Manage your feelings and reactions.

122

Middle route talents

"Everyone is smarter than me!"

"You in no manner pay attention to a few component I say!"

"You sincerely don't recognize me!"

If you have were given were given ever been worried in an issue at the aspect of your teenager that starts with this shape of polorizing statements, you will have determined it quite a mission. It may be tough in your infant to manipulate their emotions and characteristic a positive communique after transferring from rational thinking to black-and-white wondering. However, our teens aren't the best ones dealing with the demanding conditions of black and white thinking. Parenting teenagers can gift us adults with complex dichotomies along with being too strict as opposed to too lenient or linked as opposed to forcing independence. To show our children that we too face those struggles, we're able to normalize demanding situations and search for wholesome answers.

One way to understand and learn how to deal with these tough intervals of parenting is to use the metaphor of "on foot the center path."

Here are three approaches to undertake a extra dialectical manner of thinking and performing:

• Move far from "each-or" thinking to "each-and" questioning. Avoid phrases like "in no way" and "usually." Be descriptive. For example, in preference to pronouncing "we constantly have trouble," say "from time to time we have trouble speakme and special instances we speak nicely." Or, in region of saying, "You are a youngster. You want to be independent," say, "you'll be independent and ask for assist." Finally, in preference to saying, "You in no manner do your homework," say, "Sometimes you do your homework, and from time to time you forget."

• Accept that unique evaluations may be legitimate, even if you disagree with them. DBT maintains that no individual has the absolute reality, and we must be open to options. Even if we assume our teens are incorrect, it is crucial to validate what they get hold of as actual with. By validating, we display our kids that what they enjoy is vital to us. It lets in them to revel in cherished and revered.

• Check your assumptions, and don't assume others to study your mind. We can't count on we realize what's taking region in our children's heads any greater than we're capable of assume them to apprehend what's going on in ours. So we want to ask our kids clarifying questions like "Can you tell me greater about this?" We also need to try and be clean, announcing such things as, "What I'm trying to say is that I feel___ approximately ___."

Distress tolerance talents

You are surely home collectively together with your own family, however it's no longer a cushty scenario—someone within the residence has an lively consuming disorder. Intense emotions, chaos, and warfare are amplified within the house, and certainly no person can get away the anxiety and fear. Siblings are chickening out from own family life. As mother and father, you find it difficult to live in track with each other. Meals and meal coaching are a large range. Sound acquainted to you?

All parents with immoderate-threat or emotional teens want useful aid to cope with the strain related to this difficult parenting project. In difficult instances consisting of these, mother and father need to address themselves at the same time as additionally responding to the youngster in need to realize precisely a manner to assist them with out empowering the kid or making the state of affairs worse.

Emotion regulation abilties

Emotion law or self-law is the capacity to display screen and modulate one's emotions and specific and manage the ones emotions.

Parents learn how to show their youngster's triggers and emotional

126

reactions to manipulate situations at domestic and reply greater successfully to the teenager's desires. It way more stability, extra peace, heaps less strain and lots lots less battle.

If the statistics on the way to help kids expand self-law seems overwhelming, it is. It reminds us that parenting is essential in shaping our children's destiny.

Nevertheless, none people can provide a truely exceptional home, genetics, or modeling. Expecting perfection from ourselves can actually increase tension and negativity.

We need to preserve running on our emotional muscles and try to construct a supportive environment. And it's never too overdue to start.

So, located away your worries, be given yourself and your own family as you are. The strive is probably well well well worth it.

Interpersonal effectiveness competencies
This potential set allows dad and mom increase and focus on their interaction

with young adults—ensuing in plenty less emotional responsiveness and additional effective interactions at the a part of the dad and mom and adolescent. Succinctly positioned, parents feel nearer and greater related to their teen whilst putting boundaries that artwork.

HOW TO TEACH EMOTIONAL INTELLIGENCE TO TEENS

Emotional intelligence isn't always often mentioned among families or in magnificence. This is the form of conversation you will possibly have with a therapist or health trainer. While it's not often stated, it's miles a fantastic trouble for adults and teenagers. First, we want to know why our young adults lack emotional intelligence.

Parenting and upbringing patterns

Emotional mindfulness and empathy start to develop in childhood. Parents and others help form the ones skills as teens develop vintage. Children frequently increase up with higher tiers of emotional intelligence when their primary caregivers:

- Offer love and affection
- Respond speedy to their goals
- Inspire them to speak approximately their feelings and to specific them efficaciously
- Demonstrate proper emotional law capabilities

Low emotional intelligence can also stand up in families. Children whose parents have lower emotional intelligence may also moreover discover it tough to control their feelings due to the reality they have got now not located healthy confrontational abilities.

Teens also can moreover have decrease emotional intelligence if parents provide inconsistent assist and warmth, in no way encourage them to specific their feelings, or punish them for showing their emotions.

Research additionally links decrease emotional intelligence to horrible parental wondering, which can embody:

- Inconsistent place
- Excessively intense location

- Attempts to exercise control

Mental health troubles

Difficulty figuring out and controlling emotions can be a symptom of a few intellectual fitness problems, which consist of melancholy and borderline person sickness.

Low emotional intelligence can also contribute to social tension.

If a teenager has a tough time know-how how distinctive human beings revel in, they will discover interactions traumatic and be afraid to mention a few trouble that makes human beings irritated.

Persistent social anxiety can finally purpose them to keep away from social conditions and make a contribution to emotions of depression or hopelessness.

REASONS TO BECOME MORE EMOTIONALLY INTELLIGENT

If you consider emotional intelligence is simplest giant to folks that always want to have interaction or communicate with humans, assume over again. Emotional intelligence is the gateway to a balanced life. It is vital for almost all additives of life along side:

Physical fitness

The ability to attend to our frame and manipulate stress, which has an extraordinary impact on our favored well-being, is strongly connected to our emotional intelligence. Only by being aware about our emotional nation and our reactions to stress in our life are we able to want to manipulate stress and hold appropriate fitness.

Mental properly-being

Emotional intelligence influences our outlook and thoughts-set on existence. It can also assist relieve anxiety and prevent depression and temper swings. A excessive diploma of emotional intelligence is straight away associated with a pleasant attitude and a happier outlook on existence.

Relationships

By higher coping with and information our feelings, we will constructively speak our feelings. In turn, we also can better relate to and apprehend others.

Understanding the desires, emotions, and reactions of those near us results in extra sturdy and first-rate relationships.

Conflict choice

It is an awful lot a lot less hard to remedy conflicts or avoid them altogether even as we can decide people's feelings and recognize their thing of view. We are also higher at negotiating because of the very nature of statistics the wants and needs of others. It's clean to offer human beings what they want if we recognize what it's miles.

Success

Motivation is an important part of emotional intelligence; motivation builds our self-self assure, stops us from procrastinating, and allows us interest on our dreams.

It moreover lets in us to construct better assist networks, triumph over setbacks and persevere with a more resilient imaginative and prescient. Our capacity to postpone gratification and notice the prolonged-time period straight away affects our capacity to achieve success.

Leadership

Understanding what motivates others, building remarkable relationships, and forging more potent bonds within the workplace necessarily makes higher leaders of these with better emotional intelligence. In addition, appropriate leaders can recognize their employees's dreams honestly so those desires may be met. This encourages higher normal common overall performance and hobby pleasure.

An smart and emotionally savvy leader can also construct stronger groups by way of manner of the use of strategically making use of the emotional range of their participants for the benefit of the organization as a whole.

SO, HOW DO YOU TEACH YOUR TEENS EMOTIONAL INTELLIGENCE?

Teens frequently want advice on what to do with their feelings. Some teenagers have emotional u.S. Of americaand downs and won't have the gear to manipulate them. In the worst-case situation, a youngster may additionally additionally motel to capsules or alcohol to control his feelings. In special times, teens may additionally withdraw and probable even become depressed. Here are seven approaches to help your little one come to be more emotionally capable:

1. Talk approximately emotional intelligence. Perhaps the best way to begin is to train your infant about emotional intelligence and its importance. You can also look at factors or the complete of Dan Goleman's e-book Emotional Intelligence or other books at the task.

2. Practice emotional intelligence at domestic. Becoming emotionally clever takes workout. It method remembering to don't forget. Mindfulness does no longer come because you need it. It is a choice, a conscious desire to be aware about your emotions. Parents can assist their

teenagers with the aid of asking them the following questions:

• What became your first response?

• How do you feel about this?

• What fears or anxieties are bothering you?

• How did it make you experience?

• What are you passionate about?

In one-of-a-kind phrases, permit feelings to be mentioned.

3. Model emotional intelligence. Your teen can also learn how to include emotional intelligence into their life when they see you doing so. When they recognise which you are comfortable collectively in conjunction with your emotions, they will growth the ability to do the same.

four. Attend workshops or education publications together. Emotional intelligence is becoming a famous subject remember. Chances are you and your infant may additionally additionally locate an event to wait that specializes in the manner to turn out to be extra emotionally clever.

five. Let your toddler's counselor or therapist recognize that you are on foot on emotional intelligence. If your little one works with a intellectual fitness provider, it could be useful for that provider to be conscious which you and your little one exercise emotional intelligence. A therapist can in addition manual your infant's capacity to be extra emotionally aware.

6. Take an internet take a look at to determine how emotionally smart you are. You and your infant can also want to try this collectively. Take an internet take a look at to assess your capabilities and skills.

7. Involve your infant in a useful resource institution targeted on emotional intelligence. Many guide businesses are to be had to assist young adults with severa intellectual health topics. Developing emotional awareness may be taken into consideration one of them.

The seven techniques above have proved to be powerful over the years. DBT is one of the first-rate techniques to teach young adults to be emotionally wise.

DBT has helped teenagers and teens struggling with a few or all of the following:

- Frequent mood swings
- Impulsive/disruptive behaviors
- Self-injurious and suicidal behaviors
- Family and peer war
- Depression and tension
- Anger outbursts
- Drug or alcohol abuse
- Eating disease behaviors
- Poor coping skills

three

PRACTICE MINDFULNESS TO IMPROVE SELF-WORTH

H

as your thoughts ever felt like it may't close down? Different thoughts bypass spherical your head like an uncontrollable carousel. And the extra you try and avoid them, the quicker they appear to head. Yet, all you need is a few internal peace.

You've probably have a look at approximately mindfulness and the way it could lessen strain. Or maybe a friend has been extolling its virtues. You may additionally have seen a poster within the scientific doctor's place of job. It seems like a few trouble you will be interested in, a few component you need. But the same antique idea to "sit down down and watch your breath for thirty mins" is difficult, to say the least. And then you definitely definately definately play with the idea for a while, now not understanding wherein to begin. Or possibly you've even tried it numerous times, most effective to give up in frustration as your "monkey mind" chatters restlessly louder than ever.

If you keep in mind you studied you aren't the "mindfulness type," you could surrender too quickly. However, there can be a much a great deal less complex way to keep in mind. And I promise you it's far going to offer you the results you want.

I understand due to the fact I changed into there.

Some years within the beyond, I went thru a tough duration. I spent an excessive amount of time in my head, or even after I wanted to save you, I couldn't. I can also feel exhausted at the cease of each day, but my thoughts stored buzzing. I felt like I changed into going crazy. I become irritating for a way out and started studying about meditation. I moreover took education. However, for a few cause unknown, it failed to artwork for me. It changed into too difficult. It took too extended. So, I gave up.

Then, after a few months, a pal introduced me to a contemporary manner of dwelling, a manner of residing mindfully, a manner that worked for me. And it will give you the effects you need too. But, on the way to use this new method nicely, we want to first recognize what mindfulness is.

SO, WHAT IS MINDFULNESS?

Mindfulness involves being absolutely gift in the moment. It is a exercise for developing recognition and developing a greater compassionate relationship with your self. It relates to notions of internal peace, well-being and proper intellectual health. Mindfulness teaches you to locate peace inner your self. Being grounded in the present is the vital aspect to reputation. Buddhist monk, creator and mindfulness instructor Thích Nhất Hạnh states, "The modern-day second is the best time over which we've dominion."

Spending too much time daydreaming, planning, trouble-solving, or having terrible or random thoughts can be hard. Unfortunately, it is able to moreover increase the risk of experiencing stress, tension, and symptoms and signs and symptoms of melancholy. Practicing mindfulness physical activities permit you to shift your awareness far from this type of wondering and engage with the area around you.

There are numerous clean procedures to exercise mindfulness. Here are a few examples:

• Pay interest. It's hard to slow down and discern matters out in a quick-paced international. Try to make the effort to find out the surroundings with all your senses: touch, taking note of, sight, taste and scent. For example, when you devour a favourite food, take some time to scent, flavor and in reality revel in it.

• Live the immediately. Intentionally try to deliver open, responsive, and demanding hobby to everything you do. Find delight in clean pleasures.

• Accept your self. Treat yourself like an high-quality pal.

• Concentrate on your respiration. When you've got unsightly mind, strive sitting down, ultimate your eyes and taking a deep breath. Concentrate on how your breath comes interior and out of your belly. Sitting and breathing for a minute can help.

In addition, you may try greater primarily based mindfulness sports activities, together with:

• Body test meditation. Lie in your decrease back, fingers at your components, palms handling up and legs immediately. Slowly and deliberately pay interest your interest on each part of your body, from head to toe or head to toe. Be aware about any emotions, feelings or mind associated with each part of your frame.

• Sitting meditation. Sit conveniently together with your lower lower back at once, feet flat at the ground and arms in your knees. As you breathe thru your nostril, cognizance at the breath that is going outside and inside of your frame. If any concept or bodily sensation interrupt your meditation, record the enjoy, then reputation once more in your respiratory.

• Walking meditation. Find a quiet place three-six meters prolonged and slowly start on foot. Focus at the on foot revel in, being privy to the sensations of reputation and the diffused movements that preserve stability. At the stop of your set route, turn round and keep on foot, all of the on the identical time as being privy to what you are feeling.

WHY DO YOU NEED MEDITATION?

Meditation can offer you with a experience of calm, popularity and stability that might advantage your emotional properly-being. Meditation has moreover been shown to help us:
• Be heaps much less distracted
• Pay higher interest
• Learn extra
• Avoid getting dissatisfied too with out issues
• Stay calm underneath stress
• Slow down rather than dashing
• Be extra affected person
• Listen higher to others
• Feel happier and enjoy topics greater
• Get along better
• Get responsibilities completed
• Gain strength of will

Children and teens who use mindfulness may additionally expand a experience of interest about how their mind works and why they experience what they'll be feeling, in the long run primary to greater expertise of who they'll be as an man or woman. Studies have proven that after mindfulness is applied in faculties, it offers many social, emotional and cognitive benefits.

Social significance

Difficulty communicating and interacting with others can purpose problems in getting to know and statistics in the college surroundings. But mindfulness packages had been established to decorate those abilties and result in immoderate high-quality educational results.

For instance, a 5-week mindfulness software program software at an stylish college brought about higher participation in school room sports. Meanwhile, a excessive college mindfulness software helped promote mutual appreciate among university college college students.

Emotional importance

Emotional fitness is a massive a part of any infant's life. It isn't handiest the inspiration of highbrow fitness, but it is able to moreover help prevent highbrow health troubles together with:

- Fatigue
- Anxiety
- Depression
- Improved social interactions
- Self-esteem issues

Overall, paying interest or taking part in outreach sports activities sports can assist college students deal with strain and growth their experience of properly-being. For example, one examine determined that scholars have been more likely to say they had been optimistic after taking part in a mindfulness software. Meanwhile, every different have a look at located that young adults stated feeling calmer, slumbering better, and having a greater revel in of nicely-being after participating in a five-week pressure bargain and mindfulness application.

Cognitive importance

Research has set up that education mindfulness to youngsters can impact their cognitive talents, in particular the government competencies finished through manner of the mind. Executive talents are responsible for an individual's capability to pay interest, shift interest, arrange records, consider information, and plan.

HOW DOES MINDFULNESS WORK?

Mindfulness takes exercising. The amount of time spent working towards will decide how aware you are.

Mindfulness will come obviously for your every day lifestyles as you exercising mindfulness capabilities. Mindfulness decreases your strain stages and permits you stay more centered at the same time as managing complex duties.

When training mindfulness abilties, you educate your memory and attention talents. Practicing mindfulness can enhance the attention span of just about truly all of us, which consist of human beings with ADHD or those who've problem focusing.

GETTING STARTED WITH MINDFULNESS

This meditation concentrates on breath, not because it's far something precise, however because the bodily sensation of respiration is there, and you could use it as an anchor to stay within the present 2d. During breathing workout, you may discover yourself caught up in mind, emotions, sounds—anywhere your thoughts goes, come back to the subsequent breath. Even if you could most effective come once more as soon as, that's quality.

A clean meditation exercising

• Sit in reality. Find a place that offers strong, strong, and comfortable seating.

• Note wherein your legs are. For instance, if you are sitting on a pillow, skip your legs quite virtually inside the the front of you. If you are on a chair, location your ft at the floor.

• Straighten your top frame, but don't stressful your self up. Your spine has a herbal curvature. Let it's there.

• Note what your fingers are doing. First, positioned your arms parallel in your top body. Then, vicinity your arms for your legs in which they enjoy maximum natural to you.

• Soften your look. Lower your chin slightly and permit your gaze slowly drop. It makes no sense to shut your eyes however don't attention on any particular item.

• Feel your breath. Concentrate on the bodily sensation of the breath: the air passing via the nostril or mouth, the falling and developing of the chest or stomach.

• See how your thoughts wanders together with your breath. Inevitably, your interest will wander a few vicinity else. Do not fear. It isn't crucial to block or get rid of the idea. When you find your mind wandering slowly, shift your attention to the breath.

• Be kind on your wandering thoughts. You may additionally find out that your mind is typically wandering—this is additionally everyday. Instead of stopping your mind, exercising noticing them with out reacting. Sit down and pay hobby. As hard as it's far to preserve, that's it. Catch your breath numerous instances, with out judging or geared up.

• When you're ready, appearance up slowly (if your eyes are closed, open them). Take a second and feature a look at the sounds round you. Notice how your frame feels proper now. Watch your mind and feelings.

Connection among frame image and mindfulness

When it entails how we appearance, our belief of our frame can generate all kinds of mind and feelings. Unfortunately, however, for loads people, the important lens via which we see ourselves isn't a real reflected photo of the manner others see us. Even so, it's miles commonplace for lots of us to warfare with body image problems, no matter our age, size, or frame form.

As we navigate the feelings and mind we have approximately our body, the most essential barriers we're handling are just that: thoughts and emotions. Our harsh inner critic and that "not suitable sufficient" questioning can appear so loud and possibly even discouraging at instances that we're able to't pay hobby whatever else. In our journey in the direction of frame positivity, we want to regulate our thoughts-set to the ones awful mind. This is in which meditation can help.

When we workout meditation, we start to see the individual of wondering in its entirety—we get drawn into awful chatter till we apprehend how delusional the ones mind are. We are folks who offer weight and which means that to mind, so meditation teaches us to permit mind come and pass without permitting the recollections we've got got created for ourselves to have an impact on us.

When a belief pops up in our thoughts, we are capable of phrase it with out connecting with it; how frequently we attempt this determines how a exquisite deal vicinity we create in our mind, no longer only for the ebb and float of mind however moreover for self-popularity.

Practicing mindfulness to help with eating problems

For lots people, our emotions for our our bodies are often related to our relationship with food. If that earrings real, it is able to be useful to try to devour mindfully. This exercising can help us turn out to be aware about the mind, feelings, and sensations that manual our meals selections, in the long run foremost to a greater appreciation for our our our our bodies and the food we eat.

Research suggests that after humans devour extra mindfully, they might manipulate their urges to overeat, binge-eat, or eat for emotional reasons. This particular way of consuming doesn't reputation on variables like weight or calorie monitoring. Instead, we flip our hobby inward to pay attention the internal indicators and sensations our body gives us in figuring out how tons, whilst and what to devour. It moreover allows us to be present with all our senses, with out judgment.

Interpreting the relationship amongst body photo and mindfulness

What exactly do the ones discoveries inform us, and the way can they gain those enhancing from an eating disease? This research has indicated that fantastic elements of mindfulness, particularly the exercise of non-judgmental popularity, can significantly have an effect on the treatment of ingesting problems, as mindfulness can inspire popularity of someone's body and identification.

IMPROVING YOUR SELF-ESTEEM BY ACCEPTING YOUR BODY AS IT IS

Accepting your body doesn't display up in a unmarried day for maximum people. But the extra you practice gratitude and turn out to be aware of the terrible belongings you say to your self, the nearer you get to accepting your "flaws" and seeing them as part of who you are. Finding the proper network, the proper assets, and, if desired, a registered dietician or therapist can help you get started out on the right course.

When you get dressed inside the morning, don't forget of the way you reflect onconsideration on your self:

• Do you placed you would like to appearance distinct if your pants have been a length smaller?

• Do you seriously analyze the elements of your body that you are not happy with?

• Do you've got got a have a study magazine covers and constantly examine your frame to that of a version?

How you view your body will have an effect for your food selections, relationships, happiness, and common fitness via manner of addressing the daily communicate about the way you appearance and feel about your body.

Check out the ones five strategies that will help you take shipping of your body and display it extra love.

• Practice a splendid inner talk

• Choose to certainly receive your body and set practicable goals

• Stop comparing your body to others

• Focus on the extremely good elements

• Show your frame that you locate it irresistible

EFFECTS OF THE MEDIA ON BODY IMAGE

Media, social media and peer pressure have an effect on how teens see themselves. Their mental belief in their appearance can emerge as distorted, crucial them to undertake volatile behaviors after they suppose they'll be not as much as the impossible reason set for them. The impact of media on body photo can reason self-picture problems main to consuming problems, drug and alcohol use, and horrific bullying and sexual behavior.

Social media influencers, celebrities, TV, films, magazines, and the net bombard teenagers with photographs and stress concerning what their our our our bodies must seem like. The trouble is that these versions of "beauty" can't be done due to the reality they will be no longer practical. Most of the pictures are ethereal variations of models that weigh twenty-3 percentage plenty less than the commonplace lady. Yet tens of thousands and heaps of teens trust the lies and inn to unhealthy measures to try and healthy into this now not viable mould.

DEPRESSION AND NEGATIVE BODY IMAGE

A awful body picture can threaten highbrow health, however you can make a distinction through loving your body for what you may do with it as opposed to focusing on your weight or appears.

Adolescence is fraught with annoying changes, and bodily improvement can be the sort of annoying conditions, particularly if a youngster's frame does now not meet the standards of society or their very private requirements.

A new take a look at observed that a terrible body picture can threaten intellectual fitness and that youngsters disenchanted with their our bodies have a tendency to be afflicted through depression in maturity.

Research referred to in a check published in the Journal of Epidemiology & Community Health has shown that as much as sixty-one percentage of teenagers cautioned feeling disillusioned with their our our bodies. The studies additionally files this as an upward fashion correlating with the boom in social media.

As a massive rule, youngsters do no longer be stricken via despair, however the risk will boom as they grow antique. The authors consequently investigated the correlation amongst despair and frame photograph in teens.

Both ladies and boys have been slightly happy with their our our bodies in elegant, but ladies tended to be extra dissatisfied than boys. "Girls have a tendency to be disappointed with their thighs, belly and weight, and glad with their hair and hips," the authors said. "For guys, the maximum dissatisfied factors of the body were the collect, belly and hips."

Weight and frame form had been the most not unusual regions of pain: via the usage of the age of 14, fourteen percent of boys and thirty-two percentage of women have been dissatisfied with their weight. Over twenty-seven percentage of women and almost fourteen percentage of boys were unhappy with their determine. In addition, girls who've been disenchanted with their our our bodies at age 14 had mild, slight, and excessive depressive episodes at age 18, even as boys had slight or moderate depressive episodes. The findings evaluation with the belief that a negative body photo is precise to high BMI and girls and girls.

HOW TO BUILD A POSITIVE BODY IMAGE

Working on your body photograph can beautify your vanity and self warranty. Whatever you recognition on gets higher. Below are pointers to get you started out:

• Remember, our our bodies are available in all patterns and sizes.

• Don't have a look at your self to others.

• Look at all the selections you're making to be ok with yourself. It will let you begin taking advantage of possibilities you formerly prevented out of fear of your appearance.

• Donate clothes that not serve a notable purpose. Then discover fabric and colorations in that you feel right.

• When poor thoughts enter your mind, look for a save you signal. Realize that this is the mental noise of cultural judgments, feedback and comparisons.

• Handle unwanted comments approximately your frame. For example, tell them, "I should understand it if you didn't talk about my frame."

• Know that what you notice on social media is regularly now not truth.

• Regulate your intake of social media. You can discover human beings of severa ethnic and racial identities, abilities and frame kinds on social media.

• Take care of your body in a manner that makes you feel higher. Try to devour healthful meals regularly, but do now not pick out meals as "well" or "terrible." See your frame as a few thing to nourish in place of punish with restrictive nutrients or immoderate exercising.

• Feel your body as a device, now not an decoration. Focus on what your frame can do, now not on what you appear like—

this can make you more aware of how cute your body actually is.

HOW CAN MINDFULNESS IMPROVE YOUR RELATIONSHIP WITH BODY IMAGE AND FOOD?

Eating mindfully encourages us to understand what motivates our preference for food. This approach can help us become more attuned to our frame and respond to its indicators. Ideally, if we are in track with our frame, we consume at the same time as we're physical hungry; simultaneously, we want to take note of the advent, scent, flavor, and thoughts about the meals we consume. We are regularly now not bodily hungry but are responding to ancient impulses for comfort or enjoyment with meals. In that case, we have to learn how to react to the goals of our frame with extra healthful attitudes to food. There is mostly a highbrow basis that can be similarly explored with the guide of a therapist. Over time, this approach can assist us boom a wholesome dating with meals.

Mindful ingesting may be specially beneficial when you have frame picture problems or eating problems. Shift your interest out of your outer appearance to the feeling of your body at the interior. Overall, it'll will let you song into your inner strategies, signals, and emotions.

However, you want to exercise aware eating and decorate your frame, no longer because of the truth you want the recognition or approval of others, however because you want to enhance your health. It's about looking after your self and now not impressing others.

Mindfulness exercising

Let's supply it a attempt! Below is a clean mindfulness workout regarding food, in this situation, raisins. But, of direction, it can be used with any food.

• In your hand, preserve one of the raisins. Take some slow, deep breaths. Now, have a look at the raisin as if you've in no way seen one earlier than. What is its surface like? What color is it? How does it experience amongst your hands? What is its texture? What do you think about raisins or food in famous right now? Do you have any mind or feelings about whether or now not you want raisins? Assess your mind or feelings.

• Be privy to your reason to begin consuming. Slowly skip your distinctive hand inside the course of the raisins. Mentally check the movement, saying to yourself: "Reach ... Reach ... Reach." Now take the raisin and say to yourself, "Lift… elevate… lift." The reason is to be aware of every movement of your hand and arm with the beneficial useful resource of naming them.

• Now bring the raisin on your mouth and watch your hand as you do it. Smell the raisin. What does it heady scent like? How do you react to the odor? Is your mouth watering? If so, be conscious what it's far want to need to consume.

• Put the raisin for your tongue. How does it experience? Is your mouth watering?

Now bite the raisin. Where is the raisin to your mouth? Start chewing slowly. What are the sensations on your tooth? Your tongue? Which component of your tongue is experiencing the flavor? How does your tongue flow into whilst you chunk? Where is your arm? Did you examine it glide to wherein it is now?

• Then note the urge to swallow. Now swallow the raisin. Try to be aware of how the raisin movements from the oesophagus to the stomach. Can you experience a sensation in your belly? Where is your belly? What is its length? Is it empty, complete or in among? Imagine your frame is now "a hint heavier."

• Now make the effort to eat the opposite raisins with the equal degree of reputation.

Chapter 9: Being Overweight Shouldn't Stop You From Being Happy With Your Body

Many topics can purpose excess weight. People can be overweight due to genetics, manner of existence options, or hormonal imbalances. For many, being overweight should have an effect on their vanity and bodily activity. However, being obese need to not intervene with each day sports activities. You can do numerous subjects to feel good about yourself, regardless of your weight.

1. Develop Confidence
• Remember your energy
• Get inspired
• Stop evaluating yourself with others
• Use first rate affirmations
• Accept compliments
• Surround yourself with quality human beings

2. Living a complete existence
• Do some element new

• Make a listing of the topics you have not executed because of the truth you are obese.
• Embrace romance
• Wear the clothes you need regardless of what.
3. Feeling proper physically
• Choose a form of workout
• Go outdoor
• Choose a practical goal
• Play a pastime
• Get a instructor or a chum
• Join a collection or magnificence
• Check in with our medical doctor

HOW PARENTS CAN HELP TEENAGERS WITH A BODY IMAGE PROBLEM

A healthful body photograph is a exceptional a part of a teenager's developing conceitedness. Know what you can do to assist your infant sense snug with their frame.

Talking about body photo collectively in conjunction with your teenagers can assist them enjoy proper approximately themselves. When it includes frame photo, you could:

• Set an brilliant example. The manner you be given your frame and communicate of different human beings's our our our bodies can appreciably effect your little one. Remind your little one which you exercising and devour a balanced healthy dietweight-reduction plan for health, now not simply appearance. Think approximately what you watch and look at, in addition to the products you buy and the message your alternatives deliver.

• Use powerful language. Rather than speaking approximately your toddler's or distinct humans's bodily attributes, praise their non-public developments which incorporates power, staying power and kindness. Avoid commenting on lousy bodily attributes. Do now not supply or permit offensive nicknames, jokes or remarks based on someone's physical traits, body form or weight.

• Explain the consequences of puberty. Ensure your youngster is conscious that weight benefit is a wholesome and everyday a part of boom, in particular inside the direction of puberty.

• Talk approximately multimedia messages. Social media, movies, TV shows, and magazines frequently ship the message that wonderful a particular frame kind or pores and skin color is right sufficient. Maintaining an attractive appearance is the most essential goal. Media selling fitness, athletics, or fitness also can constitute the proper of a slim body—a toned, lean frame. Images from social media and magazines are also frequently altered. As a result, teens attempt to gain ideals that don't exist in the real global.

• Check and discuss what your toddler reads, browses or watches. Encourage your infant to question what he sees and hears.

• Monitor social media utilization. Children use social media and services to percentage snap shots and obtain feedback. Being aware of others' reviews can have an effect on how teenagers see themselves. Research moreover suggests that young adults' commonplace use of social media can be related to intellectual fitness and well being issues. Set rules in your toddler's use of social media and speak approximately what they post and spot.

Other strategies for selling a healthful frame picture

In addition to talking for your toddler approximately healthful body image, you can:

• Involve your toddler's medical doctor. Your infant's medical doctor permit you to set capacity frame mass index (BMI) and weight desires based mostly on average fitness and personal increase information.

• Adopt healthy consuming conduct. Teach your kids to eat a healthy and balanced weight loss plan. Offer a huge form of meals. Talk about the cons of fad diets and avoid labeling food "unique"or "terrible."

• Go in competition to bad media messages. Expose your youngsters to human beings well-known for their accomplishments, no longer their seems. For instance, watch films or read books approximately inspiring people and their staying strength in overcoming demanding situations.

• Praise the results. Help your toddler compare what he does in region of what he looks as if. Look for opportunities to praise their efforts, abilties, and accomplishments.

• Promote physical interest. Playing sports activities activities sports and one-of-a-kind bodily sports activities, in particular those that don't emphasize a particular weight or fitness, can help sell a wholesome frame image and proper self-esteem.

• Encourage excessive great friendships. Friends who receive and guide your youngster might also want to have a notable effect.

4

HOW TO USE MINDFULNESS TO OVERCOME STRESS, ANXIETY, AND ANGER

Children can substantially benefit from meditation. As they grow up, they advantage more from the opportunity to recognition completely on the existing and allow pass of all their one-of-a-kind mind.

Children aged nine and over begin to turn out to be greater aware about their thoughts, and that is wherein we are able to begin to discover specific strategies of meditating. Meditation can focus the thoughts and eliminate the flow of mind. To start this bankruptcy, we are able to answer some not unusual questions you'll in all likelihood have about meditation.

Why is meditation specifically appropriate for teenagers with tension?

Our children's brains are fatigued, and children of every age really want opportunities to take a few free time every day to loosen up and reputation. Meditation provides this damage and allows kids characteristic more successfully and in reality.

Today's youngsters commonly also have immoderate stages of stress. To assist them slow down, mother and father are encouraged to meditate with their kids, and instructors are endorsed to encompass mindfulness education into their lesson plans.

Teaching children to prevent, recognition and breathe may be one of the exceptional gives you supply them.

Are there any other benefits to meditation?

Yes. Practicing mindfulness wearing sports which encompass meditation will decorate interest simply so young adults can attention on homework and carry out higher at checks. Meditation also can assist improve self-esteem and memory, reduce excessive blood pressure, decrease the coronary coronary heart rate, and help stability the immune tool.

How do you get started out with a meditation software program?

Mindfulness skills are clean to exercise and best take a few minutes a day. Here is a cautioned meditation application to present for your teenager:

• Sit in a comfortable and snug function. Pick some aspect to attention on, like breathing or a word to duplicate in your head.

• Let's focus on respiratory. Breathe usually and take note of your respiration. Close your eyes if you need to. As you inhale and exhale, be privy to every breath. Be attentive however do no longer pressure it.

• Notice even as your thoughts wanders some distance from your breath. Are you beginning to reflect onconsideration on what to eat for lunch, or remembering to take your football tools to highschool, or thinking about that funny comic story someone knowledgeable you after math elegance? Notice that your mind is wandering and distracted. It's natural; minds continuously do this!

• Whenever you be aware your hobby wandering, lightly refocus to your respiratory. This is the way you increase interest control.

• Keep respiration, relax, be privy to your breathing. Continue to be privy to your breath every time your mind wanders. Do this for 5 mins.

Is meditation a manner to "stop wondering?"

No. Your mind is typically thinking.

The attentional tracking trouble of meditation should make it simpler for people to be aware of their mind and feelings, bearing in mind more flexibility in cognitive re-evaluation. Likewise, meditation does no longer continuously reduce bad thoughts or feelings, however interest manipulate advanced through meditation allows human beings cope with terrible thoughts greater brief.

How lengthy will it take for teens to gain the benefits of meditation?

Start small, four or 5 mins of meditation, increasing to fifteen minutes, as soon as a day, four or five instances every week. Changes can arise inside the teen's thoughts in about 3 weeks.

Teenagers are often on the cellular telephone. Can they use it for meditation? Yes. If your little one feels uncomfortable on the lookout for to meditate with you, this could be particularly useful! Many apps are available on your phone or tablet, which incorporates Calm or Headspace, which your little one can strive simply free. Your cellular cellular telephone also can function a meditation timer.

MINDFULNESS PRACTICES SHOWN TO HELP TEENAGERS ADDRESS STRESS

New studies finished through the usage of a Penn State College of Education faculty member shows that running in the direction of mindfulness sports activities sports, specifically aware respiration, may furthermore allow teens to control greater successfully with the strain in their lives.

In a massive intervention take a look at of 389 Grade 11 university students, the researchers examined a subset of nine university university college students participating in an L2B (Learning to Breathe) software; the researchers determined how L2B inspired the scholars' opinions of pressure and nicely-being and whether or not or now not they decided on to consist of mindfulness-related practices into everyday lifestyles. The immoderate college fitness class university college students completed quantitative self-evaluation measures (pre, post, have a look at-up), qualitative interviews, and open survey questions as part of the study.

Learning to BREATHE, evolved via Broderick, is a school mindfulness-based totally software program (MBP) designed for teenagers and applied in numerous contexts. The application consists of six thematic modules, taught over six, twelve or eighteen instructions, with issues derived from the acronym, BREATHE Body cognizance, Reflections, Emotions, Attention, Take it as it's far, Healthy Habits of thoughts, and Empowerment.

Program goals encompass supporting teenagers:

• Become conscious in their mind, feelings and bodily reviews

• Use mindfulness and compassionate focus on the same time as coping with distressing emotions and

• Practice the ones skills as a fixed.

In reading the test's findings, there has been some discrepancy among the quantitative and qualitative statistics that indicated the particular consequences of the intervention on the pressure ranges of the intention university college students. The quantitative facts determined that the students professional extra stress after participating in L2B. However, the qualitative records comprised treasured notion concerning the gear to be had to address pressure.

While the students within the L2B study participated in severa practices, which consist of conscious eating, aware on foot, and sitting meditation, aware respiratory modified into with the useful resource of an prolonged manner the most effective. The price of breathing whilst feeling stressed or demanding lies in redirecting emotional responses.

When we select topics, we react to them. L2B lets in us to pause simply so the autoresponder—that is regularly not the quality answer—gets hijacked.

An added advantage of conscious respiratory is its simplicity. It is a reachable exercising that students can without troubles combine each time, everywhere.

The have a have a look at moreover observed that scholars tormented by tension within the clinical melancholy variety benefited most from L2B bodily video games.

The university college students who had greater room to develop grew taller. However, neither the look at's qualitative nor quantitative statistics installed the huge effect of L2B on students' interaction with others.

MEDITATION FOR ANGER

When we get angry, we frequently assume that one of a kind people or subjects are responsible. If this had been actual, there may be not something we ought to do approximately it. However, studying to bear in mind of our emotions and reactions through guided anger meditation can assist us manage our emotions better.

Anger is one in each of our most effective feelings. It confuses us and prevents us from wondering in fact, frequently most important to tantrums. Meditation can help adjust our anger through spotting triggers in advance than they generate a terrible reaction.

HOW TO TRANSFORM ANGER

Emotions are our responses to the world round us; we tend to behave out and specific our feelings in phrases or movements. This is specifically right of the heightened emotion of anger.

Meditation, however, can teach us how to remodel the heightened emotion of anger right right into a extra reflective and powerful usa of mind.

When you are angry, close your ears, close your eyes, and try and pass back to a country of quiet and calm. Smile, no matter the reality that it takes try. Smiling relaxes masses of small muscle groups, making your face greater attractive. Sit everywhere you're and appearance deep internal. Or go out and exercise meditation while on foot. The important aspect is to water the seed of mindfulness and permit it increase in your intellectual consciousness.

Mindfulness is continuously the eye of a few aspect, definitely as anger is a feeling of annoyance or hostility towards some component. When you drink a cup of water and are conscious that you are eating a tumbler of water, it's far attention. In this situation, we are generating whole hobby of anger. As I inhale, I understand I'm angry. As I exhale, I apprehend the anger is in me. First comes the power of anger, after which comes hobby.

We do now not use mindfulness to pressure away or combat our anger however to heal it. This technique is non-dualistic and non-violent. It is non-dualistic as it recognizes that awareness and anger are a part of us. We recognise that anger is neither right nor lousy—it's far certainly strength. Do not try and suppress it or chase it away. Recognize that it has surfaced and address it. When you have got were given a belly pain, you do not get mad approximately it. You cope with it. When a mom hears her infant crying, she stops what she is doing, hugs the kid and comforts him. Then tries to apprehend why the child is crying. Mindfulness can educate us the way to understand the emotion, calm us down, and permit our emotions of the situation to influence our reaction to it.

UNDERSTANDING EMOTIONAL REACTIVITY

When we revel in forced, angry or harm, we commonly typically have a tendency to react suddenly. This is because of the fact we're in a country of combat or flight, and we have a propensity to overreact emotionally. This overreaction is emotional reactivity.

At this aspect, our perception of the situation is altered. The emotional fee prevents us from seeing the problem as it's far. Instead, we react. At this factor, there we do no longer pay attention anymore. Our emotions and defenses guide our behavior.

As we fear about what's bothering us, irritated thoughts fuel the flames till they reach the thing wherein we both venture our anger outward or try and blame others, and that is at the equal time as we need to recognize what function our thoughts plays in stoking the fireplace.

With sufficient exercise, we discover ways to control anger in preference to permitting anger to manipulate us. We moreover come to peer our anger greater in truth, know-how that it may indeed be a healthful emotion at the identical time as channeled correctly.

Healthy as opposed to risky anger

Healthy anger can be professional as a modern-day vibrant emotion centered on solving a problem or speaking an injustice. The sensation is short. Healthy anger is felt with little or no mind of revenge. It's not about being vindictive, having power, or hurting a person (bodily or verbally). Instead, it's far communicated efficaciously and honestly and then forgotten. Perhaps the clearest indicator that your anger is wholesome is whether it makes you enjoy real approximately your self and the possibility character.

Unhealthy anger produces mind of searching for to damage each other character. Feelings of anger may be so sturdy that you're feeling like you're dropping control, and that anger can be scary and threatening. You can be nice that your anger is dangerous if it hurts you and others (emotionally or bodily). Other bad symptoms and signs and symptoms embody suffering to permit go of your anger and having bad thoughts approximately yourself or others.

When anger arises, the concept is to honor it, enjoy it and be aware about it with out letting it damage us. This is the sort of skill we will benefit thru emotional law and meditation, a potential that begins with respiration, the use of a way referred to as "targeted interest."

Breath as a barometer

Breathing is a dependable barometer of approaches the frame and thoughts sense at any given time. If respiration had been an alarm, it might sound whenever we felt irritated, crushed, impatient or perhaps irritated. Fortunately, for each person's sake, "targeted interest" is a far quieter signal device.

When feelings of anger begin to amplify, it's miles as although the frame is full of warm, growing air that does not understand wherein to move; respiration will become shallower and faster. That's why we feel we would explode.

Emotional regulation starts offevolved with looking for a manner to release the ones excessive feelings via exhalation. So we cognizance on the breath and permit the body exhale deeply. And if we keep exhaling—, three, 4 or maybe 5 times if vital—the anger will deplete.

We feel anger constructing up, but we no longer frequently word while the anger is lengthy past. With exhalation, we not best launch tension, but we additionally deliberately take a look at the begin and prevent of anger. We because of this become aware about its impermanence.

It takes a few power of mind to be prone enough to simply accept and apprehend one's anger. It additionally takes staying power to take a look at your herbal exhalation this way, specifically inside the warmth of the on the spot. Nevertheless, taking note of this inner barometer may want to make a difference in how we loosen up and end up lots plenty less conscious of anger.

What does anger do to the frame?

As stated earlier, anger triggers the body's "combat or flight" reaction. Other feelings that reason this reaction consist of tension, worry, and satisfaction. The adrenal glands flood the body with strain hormones together with cortisol and adrenaline. The brain diverts blood from the intestines to the muscle mass for bodily exertion. Heart rate and blood stress growth, respiratory hastens, body temperature rises, and pores and skin sweats. The mind is sharp and targeted.

www.ingramcontent.com/pod-product-compliance
Lightning Source LLC
Chambersburg PA
CBHW062139020426
42335CB00013B/1269